REPUTATIONS

TEN YEARS AFTER

MILITARY STUDIES

STATESMEN AND SOLDIERS OF THE CIVIL WAR
  By Major General Sir Frederick Maurice

AN AIDE–DE–CAMP OF LEE, being the papers of Colonel Charles
  Marshall, sometime Military Secretary and Aide-de-Camp on the
  staff of Robert E. Lee, edited by Major General Sir Frederick
  Maurice

A GREATER THAN NAPOLEON: SCIPIO AFRICANUS
  By Captain B. H. Liddell Hart

GREAT CAPTAINS UNVEILED
  By Captain B. H. Liddell Hart

REPUTATIONS: TEN YEARS AFTER
  By Captain B. H. Liddell Hart

ATLANTIC MONTHLY PRESS PUBLICATIONS

Pétain, Haig, Foch, and Pershing at the
Château de Bombon

REPUTATIONS
TEN YEARS AFTER

BY

CAPTAIN B. H. LIDDELL HART

WITH ILLUSTRATIONS

BOSTON
LITTLE, BROWN, AND COMPANY
1928

THE ATLANTIC MONTHLY PRESS PUBLICATIONS
ARE PUBLISHED BY
LITTLE, BROWN, AND COMPANY
IN ASSOCIATION WITH
THE ATLANTIC MONTHLY COMPANY

TO

MY SON

ADRIAN JOHN

PREFACE

THESE studies have been approached essentially in the spirit of an historian. They have been treated in the manner of a portrait painter.

The moment for them has been chosen in order to achieve the closest possible reconciliation between the advantage of contemporary experience of events and personalities on the one hand, and, on the other, the evidence of the documentary records which are now available to throw light on the critical actions and discussions which influenced the course of the World War. Thus may history approximate most nearly to truth.

Over a long period I have been gathering impressions of the subjects of my portraits from men of the various countries who were in intimate and immediate touch with them during the war. From this mass of impressions, sifted and weighed in the scales of my own knowledge of the witnesses, their points of view and mental trends, the picture of each subject has gradually taken form in my own mind.

Finally, this picture has been analyzed and checked in the light of the records, official and personal, from British, French, American, Russian, Italian, German, Austrian, and Balkan sources. As these have enabled me to strike a balance between the various personal impressions, so, when documentary evidence has been conflicting, my judgment has been guided by the mental picture, inclining toward that which accords with the nature of the "subject" there revealed.

B. H. L. H.

CONTENTS

ILLUSTRATIONS

MAPS

MARSHAL JOFFRE

THE MODERN DELPHIC ORACLE

MARSHAL JOFFRE

THE MODERN DELPHIC ORACLE

Son of a village cooper to Marshal of France — such was the record of Joseph Jacques Césaire Joffre, who was born on January 12, 1852, at Rivesaltes on the eastern edge of the Pyrenees.   A man from the people and of the people, plain in character as in origin, here was surely the ideal representative of the "war to save democracy," and by him the capacity of democracy may fairly be judged.

It was a family tradition that the Joffres were originally Spanish, their name Gouffre, and that the great-grandfather of the future Marshal had crossed the Pyrenees as a political exile. He was a merchant, but the business decayed, and Marshal Joffre's father, as soon as he was old enough to work, took up the trade of a cooper. He remained a simple workman until his marriage, when he inherited a modest competence from his mother, which enabled him to become a master cooper. Joseph was one of eleven children, and was helped up the first rungs of the ladder by the system of State-aided education. Showing a leaning for mathematics and science while at the College of Perpignan, he was encouraged to try for the École Polytechnique, and, after eighteen months' final preparation in Paris, passed into the Polytechnique at seventeen, fourteenth on a list of one hundred and thirty-two, although the youngest of his "promotion."

This was in 1869, and the outbreak of the Franco-German War the next year interrupted his course. Like his comrades, Joffre was called to active service as a *sous-lieutenant* and took part in the siege of Paris — serving in one of the forts. At the close of that disastrous war he returned to finish his studies, but, passing out too low to have the option of a civil-service post, he took a commission in the Engineers.

That same year the youth who was destined to be the other great legendary figure of the World War entered the Engineers also — but in the army of France's future ally. The parallel between Kitchener and Joffre was soon strengthened, for the loss of his wife led Joffre in 1885 to seek distraction in colonial service, where so many of the leading soldiers of France, as also of England, have done their military apprenticeship — a service, moreover, which is a forge of character and leaves also its peculiar stamp on the mind. His reputation already, among his comrades, was that of a reserved and silent man, one who, although a staunch comrade, was neither easy to approach nor easy to move. These tendencies the desert naturally developed.

His first service, however, was in Indo-China; he took part in the Formosa campaign, and later

JOFFRE

spent three years at Hanoi as chief engineer in organizing the defense of Upper Tonking. General Mensier, who appreciated his value, brought him back to Paris in 1888 to a post in the directorate of engineer services. The following year he was promoted *chef de bataillon* in the railway regiment, and later became professor of fortification at Fontaine-bleau.

In 1892 he was sent out to West Africa, where he was entrusted with the task of building the railway from Kayes to Bafulabe. If the duty seemed prosaic, it was to prove the path to glory. For it was late in 1893 that Colonel Bonnier's expedition set out to extend French influence to Timbuktu, and Joffre was taken from his railway work to command a supplementary column of one thousand men — two thirds of whom were carriers and followers. Passing up the left bank of the Niger, he joined Bonnier at Timbuktu. His account of his march, afterward published, has no literary or narrative power, but it at least shows infinite care to ensure the supplies of the column and its protection from Touareg raiders. But the five-hundred-mile march would hardly have won him fame but for the disaster which befell Bonnier, whose force was surprised and cut to pieces by the Touaregs. The remnant joined Joffre, who imperturbably decided to continue his march. Such calm disregard of their efforts seems to have nonplused the Touaregs, for he was allowed to reach Timbuktu without serious interference. Here he received orders for recall to his railway building, but disregarded them and, after making his garrison assault-proof, secured the submission of the whole territory. The disaster to Bonnier had caused a sensation in France, so that the news of the way in which Joffre had promptly retrieved it created the greater reaction, and he was promoted to lieutenant colonel and officer of the Legion of Honor.

Recalled to France in 1896 to be secretary of the Commission of Inventions, he was soon sent abroad again — to construct the defenses of Diego-Suarez, in Madagascar, the new French naval base in the Indian Ocean. Here he was under the command of Gallieni, and the contact thus established between the two men was to have a far-reaching influence on the destiny of Joffre and of France. In 1900 Joffre was promoted to general of brigade, and quitted Madagascar on his appointment to command the 19th Artillery Brigade at Vincennes, whence he moved to the Ministry of War as Director of Engineers. Promoted to general of division in 1905, he remained at the Ministry of War for another year, when he was given command of the 6th Infantry Division, and later of the 2nd Army Corps at Amiens.

In 1910, while holding this post, he was nominated to the Conseil Supérieur de la Guerre, whose members are the official advisers of the Minister in peace and the higher commanders designate in case of war.

Joffre's prospective war appointment was that of head of the lines of communication, a post for which his previous career and technical knowledge clearly fitted him. Fate, however, intervened to cast him for a very different rôle, and one for which his qualifications outwardly seemed to be that he had none. He had come to fifty-eight years of age with hardly any experience in command of troops and no higher study of war. He was suddenly to be raised to chief of a general staff which had only one rival in its intensive — if not extensive — research into the conduct of large-scale operations of war. His equipment was the experience of a single little colonial expedition in early life and a technical knowledge of fortification and railway construction. If he had been able to bring the minds of this staff down out of the clouds, from their philosophical contemplation of the offensive spirit, to the solid groundwork of material conditions, the surprising experiment might have been justified. But in fact he proved merely a solid shield behind which subtler brains could direct French military policy on the path to a crevasse which they had not perceived — because they were too absorbed in military occultism to watch the ground over which their steps were taking them.

How did this astonishing appointment come about? Through a military revolt, none the less powerful because it was waged by tongues instead of arms. It found its leader and prophet in Colonel de Grandmaison, Chief of the Operations Branch of the General Staff. In the existing plan of campaign in case of war against Germany the French army was distributed in a strategic formation in depth, roughly diamond-shaped, which could be manœuvred against the enemy according to the line of invasion that he took. Its strategy was thus of an offensive-defensive nature, to let the enemy make the first move and then, through the elasticity of the French dispositions, to concentrate a powerful mass of manœuvre for a counteroffensive against his advance. But to Colonel de Grandmaison this plan was contrary to the French spirit and constituted "an almost complete atrophy of the idea of the offensive." Instead of waiting for the enemy to disclose his hand, "it is the quickness with which we engage the enemy that guarantees us against surprise, and the power of the attack which secures us against the enemy's manœuvres." De Grandmaison summed up his theory by saying, "We must not recoil before this principle, of which only the form seems paradoxical: in the offensive, imprudence is the best of safeguards." The conclusion was that, whatever the rôle of a force, there was only one mode of action — attack, which meant a headlong assault.

This theory certainly simplified the rôle of the leader, for directly an enemy was sighted he had merely to give the order, "Forward!" As General Boucher has told us, if on manœuvres any officer did not thus charge like a bull with lowered head, he was thought to be lacking in "nerve." The very simplicity of this theory combined with its appeal to the French temperament — and implicit tribute to the irresistible spirit of Frenchmen — to capture the imagination of the army. In the young who would have to stake their own lives the folly was at least tempered with a certain superb audacity, but in generals responsible for others' lives it was wholly culpable, and the only excuse is that they were afraid of being thought to be failing in nerve through increasing years.

General Michel, Vice President of the Conseil Supérieur de la Guerre, and therefore commander in chief designate, almost alone stood out against the tide, but under the existing system his prospective office did not give him power to control the doctrine of the General Staff. This dissociation of those who formed the doctrine — and the plan — in peace from the man who would have to carry it out in war caused a military crisis. As Michel was in a minority of one, the "Young Turks" carried the day, for, dominating the General Staff, they were firmly entrenched in the Ministry of War, where the political chief was a bird of passage, and the vice president of the council an outsider.

Michel was relieved of his post. Gallieni, who had opposed his views, had the good taste to decline, on the score of age and an experience mainly colonial, the succession to the man he had helped to displace. Pau was offered the post, but stipulated that he must be given powers which the Government was unwilling to grant, more especially as his clerical opinions made him suspect to politicians ever haunted by the bogey of a military *coup d'état*. Gallieni then proposed Joffre; the new Minister accepted the suggestion and, addressing an audience of journalists, declared: "With General Joffre . . . I shall strive to develop the doctrine of the offensive with which our army is beginning to be impregnated." Joffre was known to be such a good Republican and so devoid of political attachments that the Government did not hesitate to give him the combined functions of Vice President of the Conseil Supérieur and Chief of the General Staff, a duality which endowed him with control in peace and command in war. Heavy in body and intellect, he was obviously no Cassius. (Strange how stoutness inspires the politician with trust.) Screened by his massive frame, and under cover of his all-powerful authority, the "Young Turks" radically refashioned the official doctrine.

"The French Army, returning to its traditions, no longer knows any other law than the offensive. . . . All attacks are to be pushed to the extreme with the firm resolution to charge the enemy with the bayonet, in order to destroy him. . . . This result can only be obtained at the price of bloody sacrifices. Any other conception ought to be rejected as contrary to the very nature of war." To this end the training reverted to the Frederician, aiming at a discipline of the muscles, not of the intelligence, sacrificing initiative, in order, by an incessant repetition, "to develop in the soldier the reflexes of obedience." The successive tactical regulations issued during the forty-odd years of peace which separated the wars of 1870 and 1914 shed a curious light on the way the memory of pain fades — and still more of its cause. Thus it came about that the first regulations of 1875 were nearest to the reality of 1914, whereas the last of the series was framed for a battlefield on which there were no bullets.

But the delusive basis of the new tactical doctrine was solid in comparison with the foundations on which the new plan of campaign was built. This, the notorious Plan XVII was based on a double miscalculation. The initial strength of the German army was estimated at not more than forty to forty-two infantry divisions — whereas there were seventy-two — and, although the possibility of a German move through Belgium was recognized, the wideness of its sweep was utterly misjudged. The Germans were expected complaisantly to take the difficult route through the Ardennes in order that the French might conveniently smite their communications! Based on the idea of an immediate and general offensive, Plan XVII ordained a main thrust by the First and Second Armies toward the Saar into Lorraine.

On their left were the Third Army, opposite Metz, and the Fifth Army, facing the Ardennes, which were either to take up the offensive between Metz and Thionville or — if the Germans came through Luxemburg and Belgium — to strike northeast through the Ardennes at their flank. The Fourth Army was held temporarily in reserve near the centre, ready to combine with either the right or the left thrust, and two groups of reserve divisions were disposed in rear of each flank — relegation to such a passive rôle expressing French opinion on the capacity of reserve formations.

For the immediate cause of General Michel's downfall had been that, foreseeing the wide German sweep through Belgium, he had proposed to swell his forces by incorporating the reserve divisions in the active army. Such an idea was anathema to the "Young Turks," who held that their cherished *offensive à outrance* could only be carried out by rigidly disciplined troops whose reflexes would carry them forward in spite of bullets. Thus the way was paved for the great, and almost decisive, opening surprise of the war — for the Germans, in contrast, had not hesitated to build up their attacking mass from an amalgam of active and reserve divisions, and thus obtained a superiority of three to two at the outset. And thus the pit was dug for the downfall of Plan XVII, and almost of France, by the hands of Joffre, guided by the minds of his entourage.

The phrase, if hard, is justified not only by unofficial evidence but by the words of Joffre himself before the court of inquiry which in 1919 investigated the causes of the loss in 1914 of the Briey iron fields — whence came practically all the iron-ore supplies of France. It is, incidentally, a further side light on the narrow outlook of the French Command that their plan had not taken into account the defense of their vital economic sources.

No more pitiable disclosure of puppetry has ever been made than in Joffre's evidence. When asked to produce the plan of campaign, he first replied that he had no remembrance of it, and fatuously said: "A plan of operations is an idea which one has in one's head, but which one does not commit to paper." This was so absurd, as well as contrary to the evidence of all the other generals, that the president of the court expressed surprise that there were no traces of a plan in writing. Joffre replied, "There may be some, but it was not I who drew them up." He became more and more confused under examination and ultimately said, "You ask me a mass of things which I cannot answer; I know nothing about them."

His slow wits, combined with his inexperience of higher war study, made him a modern Delphic oracle, the mere mouthpiece of a military priesthood among whom de Grandmaison was the leading intellectual influence and de Castelnau the acting high priest.

On Joffre's appointment, his ignorance of European warfare had been officially recognized by the nomination of General de Castelnau as his assistant, and chief of staff in case of war, and although this was subsequently changed to command of an army, owing to political distrust of de Castelnau's clerical sympathies, he remained the chief influence on Joffre until the war came. As it was Pau who discounted the value of reservists, so it was de Castelnau who underrated the danger of a German advance through Belgium and neglected the fortress defenses, saying, "These strong places cramp me and take too many men. I don't want them."

When the war came, a still more astonishing revelation of Joffre's surrender of his military conscience occurred at the conference of army commanders on August 3, 1914. General Dubail, commanding the First Army, declared that he would need strong reënforcements for his 7th Corps which was to begin the offensive in Alsace. Joffre merely replied: "This plan is your plan; it is not mine." Dubail, thinking he had not been understood, began to explain his needs, whereupon Joffre, his face beaming with his usual large smile, repeated his words. The conference broke up without further light, and it was little wonder that some of the army commanders were uneasy, asking each other if there was any idea behind the massive forehead of their commander in chief.

Nor did enlightenment as to their own misconceptions come quickly either to Joffre or to his staff. On August 6, when the German guns were battering at the outer defenses of Liége, Joffre informed the French armies that "it may be concluded that the Germans are executing a plan of concentration, drawn up two years ago, of which we have knowledge." The reference was to a document found, according to the General Staff story, by a French officer, when traveling in Germany the year before, in the lavatory of his railway carriage!

Thus, in blind ignorance and supreme disdain for the enemy's moves, the main French advance into Lorraine began on August 14 — and on August 19 and 20 was broken in the Battle of Morhange-Saarburg, where the French discovered to their surprise that the material could subdue the moral, and that in their enthusiasm for the offensive they had blinded themselves to the defensive power of modern weapons, a condition which was to throw out of balance the whole mechanism of orthodox warfare.

Faced with this repulse and the now unmistakable news of a German advance through Belgium, Joffre and Company, Limited, were forced to readjust their plan, which had, it is true, partially allowed for such an alternative. But as the plan only recognized the hypothesis of a German advance east of Liége and the Meuse, and not the wider arc the Germans were actually traversing, the French Command were more than ready to believe that the enemy was merely "conforming to plan" — the French plan.

Grasping once again at phantoms, Joffre and Company embraced this idea so fervently that they transformed their counter into an imaginary *coup de grâce*. Their Third and Fourth Armies were to strike northeast through the Ardennes against the rear flank of the Germans advancing through Belgium. The left-wing (Fifth) Army, under Lanrezac, was moved farther to the northwest into the angle formed by the Sambre and Meuse between Givet and Charleroi. With the British Expeditionary Force coming up on its left, it was to deal with the enemy's forces west of the Meuse, and then to converge upon the supposed German main forces in conjunction with the "right fist" attack through the Ardennes. Here was another pretty picture — of the Allied pincers closing on the unconscious Germans! Curiously, the Germans had the same idea of a pincerlike manœuvre, with rôles reversed, and with better reason.

The worst flaw in the French plan was that the Germans had deployed half as many troops again as they had been credited with, and for a vaster enveloping movement. The French, pushing blindly into the difficult Ardennes country against a German centre supposedly denuded of troops, blundered head on into the advancing German Third and Fourth Armies, and were heavily thrown back in encounter battles around Virton-Neufchâteau. Fortunately the Germans were also too vague as to the situation to exploit their opportunity.

But to the northwest the French Fifth Army and the British had, under Joffre's orders, put their heads almost into the German noose. The masses of the German First and Second Armies were closing in on them from the north, and the Third Army from the east. Lanrezac, the French Fifth Army commander, alone had an inkling of the hidden menace.

All along he had suspected the wideness of the German wheel, and it was through his insistence that his army had been allowed to move so far north. It was due to his caution in hesitating to advance across the Sambre, to the arrival of the British on his flank unknown to the German Intelligence, and to the premature attack of the German Second Army, that the Allied forces fell back in time and escaped from the trap.

At last Joffre realized the truth, and the utter collapse of Plan XVII. An Olympian calm was his greatest asset, and with a cool resolution, admirable, if astonishing, in face of the disaster to which he had led France, he sanctioned a retirement which had already begun, while he and his staff were evolving a new plan out of the wreckage. He decided to swing back his centre and left, with Verdun as the pivot, while forming a fresh Sixth Army to enable the retiring armies to return to the offensive.

His optimism might have been again misplaced but for German mistakes. The first was the folly of Moltke, Chief of the German General Staff, in detaching seven divisions to invest Maubeuge and Givet, and to watch Antwerp, instead of using Landwehr and Ersatz troops as in the original plan. This had been drawn up as far back as 1905 by Moltke's great predecessor, Graf von Schlieffen, who had decided on the route through Belgium, and whose governing idea had been to mass overwhelming strength in the wide-marching right wing. He had even welcomed the likelihood of a French advance into Lorraine, and made his left wing there purposely weak, for thus the action would be like a revolving door — the more heavily the French pressed on the east side in Lorraine, the more effectively would the western side in Belgium swing round and hit their exposed rear. Schlieffen's dying words were: "It must come to a fight, only make the right wing strong."

A more ominous infringement of his plan was when, on August 25, 1914, Moltke decided to send four divisions to check the Russian advance in East Prussia. All these were taken from the right wing, and the excuse afterward given for this violation of the principle of concentration was that the German Command thought that the decisive victory had already been won!

Further, the German headquarters lost touch with

the advancing armies and the movements of these became disjointed. The British stand at Le Cateau and Lanrezac's riposte at Guise were also factors in checking the German enveloping wing, and each had still greater indirect effects. For Le Cateau apparently convinced the German First Army commander, Kluck, that the British army could be wiped from the slate, and Guise led Bülow (Second Army) to call on Kluck for help, whereupon the First Army wheeled inward, thinking to roll up the French left. The idea of a new Sedan was an obsession with the Germans, and led them to pluck the fruit before it was ripe. This premature wheel before Paris had been reached was an abandonment of the Schlieffen plan, and exposed the German right to a counterenvelopment.

While the French Command clung too long to preconceived ideas, the Germans could not cling long enough to any idea. Almost daily during the advance they were changing their minds, — and the original plan, — until on September 4 they definitely abandoned it in favor of a concentric thrust on both sides of Verdun, which was intended to squeeze the French armies as in a pair of pincers. One further factor must be mentioned, perhaps the most significant of all: the Germans had advanced so rapidly that their supplies failed to keep pace. Thus, in sum, so much grit had worked into the German machine that a slight jar would suffice to cause its breakdown. This was delivered in the Battle of the Marne.

The reputation of Joffre is so linked with the drama of 1914 that it is essential to paint his figure against a background of events, but we have here reached a point at which we can break off for a brief sketch of his personal action during the great retreat.

It is beyond doubt that he did much by his moral — rather than by his mental — influence to repair the shattered fighting power of France. This influence was applied, not by any soul-stirring appeal, but by simply visiting the headquarters of his sorely tried subordinate commanders and sitting there, saying little, but conveying such an impression of ponderous and benign calm that they felt that affairs must be favorable elsewhere, however serious was their own situation. By similar intervention he sought to pour oil on the troubled relations between Sir John French and Lanrezac, and to secure some coöperation between their two armies on the Allied flank, which were each "ganging their own gait."

More disputable is Joffre's action in dismissing several score of generals, including Lanrezac, during the retreat, which was mainly due to the blind folly of Joffre himself and his staff.

It was bitterly said later that it was fatal to offer suggestions to Joffre and to prove right when he was wrong; that Lanrezac was "sacked" because he divined the German plan; Ruffey (Third Army) because he had proclaimed the vital need for heavy artillery; Sarrail — Ruffey's successor — because he proposed sending troops by sea to Dunkirk to strike the enemy's open flank. Although Joffre's known jealousy of possible rivals lends weight to this charge, it is not the whole truth.

Lanrezac's is the most famous case. For long recognized as the ablest manœuvre general in the French army, he, like Gallieni, had distrusted the new Plan XVII, but his observations had no effect. As soon as Liége was attacked he urged that his army should be moved farther to the northwest as a precaution, but was curtly answered "that the responsibility of stopping a turning movement [by the Germans] did not rest with him." The rebuff did not quiet him, and day after day, as the news of German movements became clearer, he pressed his point. At last, on August 15, he received permission, but still with the promise that he must hold himself ready to march by the Ardennes — to the northeast! But for his insight and insistence the German right wing must have swept almost unopposed to victory; although Lanrezac had moved seventy-five miles farther west, he was still overlapped by the German right wing. And in face of emphatic orders Lanrezac, by his refusal to cross the Sambre and attack, alone prevented his army from putting its head into the German noose. The fact that he proved right was not likely to lessen the irritation of the Higher

Command at his importunity and disregard of their orders. All the public evidence strengthens the view that the man who unquestionably saved France was dismissed, at the end of the retreat, for his presumption.

But the intimate evidence of members of his staff raises a doubt. They say that this man, so acute of vision and intelligence during the concentration period, became hesitating and flustered when the German forces were actually met, and lost his nerve as the pressure increased. Did his subaltern impressions of the *année terrible* of 1870 rise again to flood his mind? It may be significant that he was born in the West Indian island of Guadeloupe. It is at least certain that he only counterattacked at Guise — a tactical victory which had a great indirect effect — under pressure from Joffre. Moreover, his friction with Sir John French made impossible that coöperation between the Allies which was vitally important. At their first meeting at Rethel, Lanrezac acquired such a contemptuous opinion of French's military knowledge that he never troubled to return the visit and made no effort to maintain liaison — making his plans as if no British troops existed on his flank.

Joffre attempted to reconcile French and Lanrezac, but in vain, and his final step in replacing Lanrezac by Franchet d'Espérey may have been justified by the need for better coöperation and unflinching determination in the forthcoming counteroffensive. It is just also to say that Joffre had a long-standing admiration and personal regard for Lanrezac, and his reluctance during several days to take the actual step of dismissing Lanrezac is supporting evidence that his action was not merely pique.

The curtain was now to rise on the immortal drama of the Marne, that battle so indecisive in its fighting, yet one which by its mere frustration of the German plan changed the whole face and issue of the war. On the morrow of the battle the German armies, although undefeated, had lost the war.

It was natural that an event which caused such a miraculous change in the course of the struggle should be explained by appropriate stories, but the documented records of the two sides now enable us to disentangle fact from fiction. The popular legend was that, following upon a check on the frontier due to mere weight of adverse numbers, Joffre conducted a masterly strategic retreat — *reculer pour mieux sauter* — and then, after drawing the Germans on to the position intended, launched his premeditated counterstroke at the chosen moment. His order of August 25 was quoted to buttress this legend. It ran thus : —

"As it has not proved possible to carry out the offensive manœuvre which had been planned, the object of the future operations will be to reconstitute on our left flank with the Fourth and Fifth Armies, the British Army, and new forces drawn from our right, a mass capable of resuming the offensive while the other armies hold the enemy for the time necessary. A new group will be formed in the neighborhood of Amiens. . . ."

This order merely discloses a fresh burst of ill-timed optimism, for it was issued at the outset of the forced retreat, before Le Cateau and other rearguard battles had revealed the full degree of the German pressure. Official orders are commonly worded with a vagueness which will cover the issuing authority in case of failure, but this one spoiled its general airiness by the incautious reference to a concrete locality — Amiens. With the retreat gathering momentum like a rolling stone, this suggested line of resistance was soon passed and the mirage of a French offensive vanished like its predecessors. A week later, on September 1, Joffre issued orders which, while still suggesting airily an ultimate counteroffensive, revealed a different outlook in the concrete details, by directing a continuance of the retreat southward and indicating the line of the rivers Seine, Aube, and Ornain as the possible limit of the retirement. Such a line well to the southeast of Paris not only left the capital exposed but was far from a good jumping-off place for any counterstroke.

But in order to know how remote in Joffre's mind was the idea of an early return to the offensive we need not rely merely on these orders. There is

ample indirect evidence. For on August 30 Joffre —
yielding to the pressure of a Government alarmed at
seeing him abandon Paris, by his direction of retreat
— detached Maunoury's Sixth Army to reënforce
the garrison of the capital. This was the newly
formed army that Joffre had assembled near Amiens,
and parting with it meant, obviously, parting with
any early hope of a counterstroke. For, once his
retreat had taken him south of the Marne, he would
be too far away for the garrison of Paris to coöperate,
even if its independent commander were willing.
And on September 2 Joffre rejected the suggestion of
Sir John French that the Allies should make a stand
on the Marne, saying: "I do not believe it is possible
to consider a general action on the Marne. But I
hold that the coöperation of the English Army in the
defense of Paris is the only course that can yield an
advantageous result."

When Joffre's supporters say that the idea of a
counteroffensive was at the *back* of his mind, the
historian can agree! The opportunity was first appreciated not by Joffre but by Gallieni, the newly
appointed governor of Paris, under whose orders the
Sixth Army had come. On September 3 Gallieni
realized the meaning of Kluck's wheel inward, realized that the flank of the German advance had thus
exposed itself to a stroke from Paris, and next day
with some difficulty won Joffre's agreement to such
action. So marked were Gallieni's initiative and

foresight that before gaining Joffre's sanction he had begun to reënforce Maunoury and had ordered the latter to make his reconnaissances and dispositions for the advance.

Even then Joffre was slow to comprehend and nearly marred Gallieni's conception by directing that Maunoury's attack with the Sixth Army should be made south of the Marne, where he would have lost the essential value of his position on the German flank — for an enveloping manœuvre. Fresh arguments on the telephone led Joffre, on the evening of September 4, to adopt Gallieni's scheme and, in combination with the flank thrust, to order the whole left wing to turn about and return to a general offensive from Verdun westward, fixing the date for September 6. But the delay robbed the attack of immediate British support; despite Gallieni's direct appeal Sir John French decided to continue his retreat for want of contrary orders from Joffre, and on September 5 he marched southward again. When he retraced his steps on September 6, it was at so leisurely a pace that Kluck was able to draw off two army corps from this sector to reënforce his menaced flank and check Maunoury's enveloping move. On the other hand, this lateral "stretching" created the gap in the German front which enabled the French Fifth Army (now under Franchet d'Espérey) to drive in the bared flank of Kluck's neighbor, Bülow, and it was this danger,

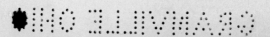

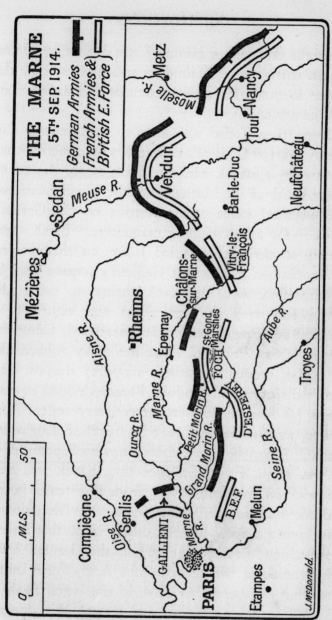

THE MARNE

combined with the feared entry of the British into the gap, which caused the German order to retreat. The onrush of the "irresistible" German war machine, already breaking down, was finally dislocated by this jar.

The most marvelous feature of the "miracle of the Marne" was its evidence of human frailty — for a month the rival commands had been outbidding each other in folly. The popular version, fostered energetically by Joffre's staff, reveals also how true to human nature is the proverb, "All's well that ends well."

Nevertheless, in justice to Gallieni's memory, it is right to emphasize other features. As he had inspired the counterstroke, so during the crucial days Gallieni rushed troops by every possible means — including the Paris taxicab — to back up Maunoury. Joffre, in contrast, not merely failed to mass troops on the decisive wing, — rather he held them back in face of Gallieni's importunity, — but on the morning of September 8 removed Maunoury's army from Gallieni's control and so checked both the flow of supports from the Paris garrison and Gallieni's efforts to exploit the opportunity of a great victory. And if Joffre had to thank Gallieni for forcing his hand, he had to thank Sarrail, commanding the Third Army, for staying his hand — by holding on to the vital pivot of Verdun in spite of Joffre's earlier instructions for retreat.

Thus, in sum, the Battle of the Marne was a strategic but not a tactical victory; and, given a respite from the initial pressure, the Germans recovered from their momentary confusion, standing firmly on the line of the Aisne eastward.

Here was reëmphasized the preponderant power of modern defense over attack, primitive as were the trench lines compared with later years. Then followed, as the only alternative, the successive attempts of either side to envelop the other's western flank, a phase known as the "race to the sea." The French, however, in the phrase of one of their own commanders, were always "twenty-four hours and an army corps behind the Germans." When the race neared its limit — the Channel coast — Joffre was wise enough to send Foch as his deputy to coördinate the Allied action. With the ultimate, but perilously narrow, success of the Allied resistance at Ypres and the Yser, trench warfare settled in and the whole front of the Swiss frontier to the sea was locked rigidly henceforth. Joffre's first attempt to unlock this barrier was expressed in the historic phrase, "*Je les grignote* (I am nibbling them)." If it was certainly no more effective than a mouse nibbling at a steel safe, the teeth it wore down were the fighting forces of France.

When this attrition-of-oneself strategy became unpopular, a variant was tried in the abortive offensives of May and September 1915 in Artois and

Champagne. But it was idle to expect from Joffre
a quick perception of the new conditions of warfare,
far less any lead or ingenuity in divining a solution.
When Colonel Carence, head of the Intelligence at
the Ministry of War, came to him early in 1915 to
plead the obvious need for heavy artillery, Joffre
gave him a patient hearing, making no attempt to
stem his flow of arguments. At first encouraged,
Carence's tide of argument finally ebbed from sheer
lack of response, whereupon Joffre gave him a
friendly pat of dismissal and the enigmatic comment,
"You always loved your guns; that's excellent."

I am reminded, too, of the anecdote told me by a
French officer, later distinguished, who some years
before the war was appointed to the "English" section of the Intelligence at the Ministry of War.
Going to pay his respects to Joffre, he was disconcerted by the great man's prolonged silence. At
last, after a series of grunts, Joffre remarked, "You
are in the English section?" Further silence; then,
"Ah, well. They used to be our enemies; now they
are our good friends. Good-bye." What an oracle!

Here we may turn to study the man in his new
surroundings — as created by the trench-warfare
stalemate. From his headquarters — the famous
G. Q. G. — near the Chantilly race course, Joffre
kept one eye on the front and the other — as well
as both ears — on Paris, for in a man so devoid of
political interests his interest in politicians was as re-

markable as his skill in dealing with them, ever alive
to incipient intrigues and quick to counteract them
through his faithful entourage and press supporters.
And to the politicians his personal reticence and spar-
ingness of phrase — here his parsimony was an asset
— formed a protective screen which baffled their
subtler wits and tongues. He had, too, the political
gift of compromise to smooth over a rough period, and
several times conciliated opposition by the prompt
transfer of an assistant to a distant sphere of activity.
Let it be said that the sacrificed ones usually took their
demission in good part — for the good of the "Company." Similarly he made a concession to political
demands in 1915 by giving countenance to the
Salonika expedition, which he had formerly opposed.
Although this support was superficial rather than
genuine, his change of attitude weakened the military opposition to this move, and disconcerted the
British General Staff, who were left to play a lone
hand in opposition.

If his long tenure of command in face of widespread
dissatisfaction was partly due to his native shrewd-
ness, it was due still more to the world-wide prestige
won him in popular opinion by the "miracle of the
Marne." For if his attendant "priesthood" had
done little to produce the miracle, they were as
prompt as their kind to exploit the opportunity and
to foster the legend. To the Villa Poiret, the shrine
of the "Savior of France," poured a ceaseless stream

of adulation and presents from faithful worshipers in all parts of the world. Pierrefeu, writer of the official communiqué, has opened to us a peephole into the inner sanctuary, disclosing delightful aspects which the contemporary historian is able to confirm and supplement from other members of Joffre's entourage. How the placid Olympian "sniffed appreciatively at this incense," shutting himself up to peruse the letters and sample the presents, signing punctiliously the replies in acknowledgment. He was the better able to spare the time because, like a model commander, he left all military details to his staff and only gave the big decisions. His office table was unencumbered by notes or papers, his walls bare of maps — except when, on the visit of a photographer, a supply was hastily brought to festoon the walls and provide a background appropriate to the popular conception.

His hold on the public was enhanced because, although remote, he was yet so akin — the very type of the *bon bourgeois*. His universal nickname, "Papa Joffre," was not only witness to his hold on the affections of the people, but symbolical of the picture he presented in the popular imagination. Simple in manner and taste, he kept a strict check on his household accounts, but relished his meals with all the gusto of a true French *rentier*, and valued his sleep. His staff learned that it was better to sacrifice duty than to be late for meals, and only in emergency would they dare to rap on his locked door after he had retired to bed — at ten o'clock.

Yet, laughable as these traits may seem in a neo-Napoleonic figure, they had the value of making him a calming influence among a race who tend to be excitable — and calm in emergency, even if it springs from insensibility, is a priceless asset. Moreover, if he was swayed by the nimbler brains of his staff officers in the technique and theory of warfare, he was indisputably master, as dominant as he was obstinate, not only in the domestic sphere but on broad questions of policy. "Thrice-armed is he who is forewarned," and Joffre, adept at frustrating political threats, was quickly suspicious of rival stars in the military firmament and jealous for his authority.

The Battle of the Marne had barely been launched before he had skillfully checked the opportunity and potential ambitions of Gallieni, the quondam superior to whom he owed his present chieftainship. And he was quick to monopolize the public glory of that victory. But he overreached himself when a year later he sought to settle the growing controversy by a "citation" of Gallieni's services which was at least a perfect example of faint praise: "Placed on September 2 under the orders of the Commander in Chief, he gave proof of the highest military qualities . . . in facilitating, by all the means in his power, the fulfillment of the mission assigned by the Commander in Chief to these mobile forces." Little wonder that this minimized recognition disgusted those who knew the truth.

This trait, moreover, paved the way for disaster — at Verdun in the spring of 1916. Like Paris, the frontier fortresses were not under the command of the chief of the field army, but instead their governors were directly responsible to the Ministry. During 1915 Joffre, who since the rapid fall of Liége and Namur had no trust in his old love, persuaded the Government to declass Verdun as a fortress, and, having won control, thenceforth drained it of its men and armaments. This removal of guns continued until a month before the German onslaught, and the casemates were simply used as shelters for troops. It was a grim jest of fate that the forts thus discarded which fell into German hands — Douaumont and Vaux — should have withstood over six months' intense bombardment from the French, the underground cover intact and not one field-gun turret destroyed.

General Coutanceau, the governor, had not shared this hasty assumption that permanent forts were valueless, but when, before a Parliamentary delegation, he dared to express his opinion, in contradiction to the Army Group Commander, General Dubail, he was not only rebuked but dismissed. Unhappily, also, the alternative defenses were neglected. Instead of an all-round defense, a single trench position was dug, and in rear only one subsidiary trench line was usable. This continuous front the new commander had not enough men or material to garrison, or to keep in an efficient state of repair.

Rumors percolated through to Paris, and in December Gallieni, now Minister of War, wrote to Joffre asking for information as to the defenses, and an assurance that they would be developed. Joffre's reply might well be framed and hung in all the bureaus of officialdom the world over — to serve as "the mummy at the feast." Rebutting the suggestions, he continued, "But since these apprehensions are founded upon reports which allege defects in the state of the defenses, I request you to . . . specify their authors. I cannot be party to soldiers placed under my command bringing before the Government, by channels other than the hierarchic channel, complaints or protests concerning the execution of my orders. . . . It is calculated to disturb profoundly the spirit of discipline in the Army." The Germans were soon to dispel his doctrine of infallibility, as the mutinies of 1917 were to show that the incapacity of generals and their waste of human life are the most potent factors in disturbing the spirit of discipline.

If the claim of Joffre and his supporters to the credit of the Marne, on the ground that he bore the responsibility, be considered just, by that same standard he is convicted for Verdun. Actually his Intelligence branch gave early news of the German preparations, but the Operations branch was so full of its own offensive schemes that the warning fell on deaf ears. Only at the last moment were adequate reënforcements sent. As the German blow had been intended for February 13, Verdun was only saved by "General Rain," who held up the attack until the twenty-first. Even when the news of the crumbling front came through, Joffre was not moved, much less disturbed. At last, on the evening of February 24, General de Castelnau — who, since his appointment as Chief of the French General Staff, had been sidetracked so far as possible by Joffre's ever zealous, and jealous, staff — took the initiative and, going direct to Joffre, gained his permission to send Pétain's Second Army to take over the defense of Verdun.

Still more alarming reports came in later, and at eleven o'clock de Castelnau, with greater daring, insisted on the orderly officer disturbing Joffre's slumbers. Before the great man returned to his bed, he gave de Castelnau authority to go to Verdun with "full powers." And in the months-long struggle which followed, Joffre and Verdun became twin symbols for patient and heroic endurance. But the French defenders lost three men to the attacking Germans' two, and the drain on the French reserves almost bankrupted their share in the long-planned Allied offensive on the Somme. Although the French fared better than their allies, the bitter cost for small gain of that long-drawn-out attrition battle sealed Joffre's fate, for he belonged to a nation which because of its more widespread military knowledge was more militarily critical. His star had deserted him; this time he did not acquire borrowed laurels from the brilliant autumn ripostes of his subordinates at Verdun, and the failure to safeguard it originally was now fully known. He had been retained in power through the summer mainly as a symbol to sustain the public confidence. As quick as ever to perceive the signs of the rising storm, Joffre sought to propitiate the angry gods by throwing overboard Foch, who had been in direct charge of the French action on the Somme, and this led to a tempestuous scene between the two. Although the sacrifice was of no avail ultimately, the Government at first thought of securing Joffre's demotion by the conventional method of promotion. They gave Joffre the new-coined title of " Commander in Chief of the French Forces," whose duty would be to act as technical adviser to the Government in the general conduct of the war. This enabled them to bring Nivelle — in public eyes the hero of the Verdun counterstrokes — to G. Q. G. to take charge of the Western Front as "Commander in Chief of the Armies of the North and Northeast." But a few days later they changed their minds again, or, perhaps relieved by the absence of public outcry at the first step, gained confidence to make a bolder change. On December

27, 1916, Joffre was definitely retired and in compensation and recognition promoted to Marshal — the first Marshal of the Third French Republic.

Pierrefeu has exquisitely painted the final scene — how Joffre summoned his staff to say farewell, and asked who would accompany him as the three orderly officers to which his rank entitled him. Only one, the much abused but ever faithful Commandant Thouzelier, raised his hand. Joffre made no complaint, but, when all had gone, turned to the loyal one and, giving him a friendly pat, uttered his favorite exclamation: "Poor old Joffre! Damned old Thouzelier!"

And by a paradox of fate the passing of Joffre, combined with the subtle manœuvre of Ludendorff, was to throw out of gear the Allied plan of 1917, leading France to fresh disaster, worse than any of those, save the first, to which his régime had contributed. In retirement, too, his help to the Allied cause was greater than in his activity, for his mission to the United States in 1917 was a triumphal procession, and as a symbol of France unconquerable he inspired Americans both with enthusiasm for the war and with a sympathy for France which for long counteracted the sources of friction.

Joffre's was not a character which lends itself to an extensive summing-up, for his virtues were primarily passive. His passivity, like his silence, was carried to such a pitch that he was one of the greatest of human enigmas. This was an inestimable asset in a world where the myth of the "strong silent man" had not yet been exploded. Reluctant to believe that a man in so great a position could be as simple as he appeared, that his superhuman calm could come from insensibility, his silence from ignorance, even the Allied leaders who met him at close quarters felt there must be unplumbed depths in the apparent shallows.

That he had real strength, or at least solidity of character, is unquestionable, as is also his possession of a shrewd if limited common sense and an instinctive understanding of human nature. And because in a time of emergency outward impressions are more important than reality, Joffre's stolid calm and obstinate determination had an influence which offset many of his grave blunders. If his brain was as solid as his appearance, lacking in flexibility and imagination, his external effect on the minds of others enabled him to become the rock on which France held and Germany foundered. Only as the documentary records come to light and the need for moral prophylactics is replaced by the need for reality, so that future generations may profit by the experience of the last, can the historian come to a more penetrating verdict. Joffre was not a general, but a national nerve sedative.

ERICH VON FALKENHAYN
THE EXTRAVAGANCE OF PRUDENCE

ERICH VON FALKENHAYN

THE EXTRAVAGANCE OF PRUDENCE

No man in all history has controlled such vast forces as Erich von Falkenhayn, and on his qualities and limitations, more than on those of any other man, turned the issue of the greatest — in scale — of all wars. He was born on September 11, 1861, at Burg Belchau in the district of Thorn, now ceded to Poland. It is a strange requital of fate that the birthplaces of the two greatest directors of Germany at war, Falkenhayn and Ludendorff, should both rest now on alien soil. Entering, through the cadet schools, an ordinary line regiment, he was singled out for distinction when he passed out from the Kriegsakademie in 1890, third of his class. Six years later he went to the Far East as instructor to Chinese troops, selected as a missionary in propagating the gospel of German world-power and as an agent in the plan of converting China into a useful military ally, with a view to the future. But the method which succeeded in Turkey was a failure in China. It would even seem from his later career that, instead of impressing German military ideas on China, he allowed the Chinese doctrine of war to gain a hold on himself.

He served on the staff of the German Expeditionary Force in the Boxer troubles, and then, returning to Germany, spent three years in command of a battalion and five years as chief of staff of an army corps. Suddenly, early in 1911, he was promoted to command a Guard regiment, a move of great significance. To soldierly gifts and the subtlety of a courtier, Falkenhayn now added a social hall mark which was almost essential to attain high position under the régime of William II. With Falkenhayn the effect was magical, for two years later he was promoted lieutenant general and became Minister of War. Such a rise at the early age of fifty-one was an astonishing tribute to his ability and influence. For in the German army youth might wield the power behind the throne, but the nominal authority and the posts of high distinction were customarily reserved either for royalty or for old age, so old that it verged sometimes on senile decrepitude.

The Kaiser has much to answer for, but from a strictly German point of view his worst sin was perhaps that by his lack of military judgment and by his military selections he undermined the strength of Germany's armed power, and so prepared her downfall. The more one studies the history of the war, the more does one realize how many times she had victory almost within her grasp, and that only through crass incapacity and, still more, lack of character at the top, did she forfeit the repeated

FALKENHAYN

chances. The greatest military machine ever created was in the hands of men morally and physically, even more than mentally, unfitted for the control. William II undoubtedly thought more of birth than of ability in making his selections, but in some cases this tendency seems to have been due more to an almost superstititous belief in heredity than to a partiality toward the aristocracy. True, he liked to have a flattering and subservient entourage, and, with an overweening conceit of his military knowledge, expected deference to his views on matters martial. Even the great Graf von Schlieffen, Chief of the General Staff from 1891 to 1906, from whose brain came the German war plan of 1914, felt the necessity of pandering to this weakness: he issued instructions for manœuvres and war games which stated that "when the Kaiser takes part he must be allowed to win; he cannot as Kaiser be beaten by one of his generals."

On the other hand, Schlieffen's successor, Helmuth von Moltke, although a weaker and inferior mind, actually restrained the Kaiser's military vanity, and was less a pliant courtier than is commonly supposed. That he was able to do so, may have been due to the fact that he was essentially the Kaiser's own choice in defiance of public opinion. Nearly thirty years of his career had been spent in the gilded post of aide-de-camp to his uncle, the great Moltke of the 1866 and 1870 wars, and to the Kaiser. Thus when in 1904 he was suddenly raised to real responsibility as one of the two Deputy Chiefs of the General Staff, the army realized that such a step must have some future significance. Their perplexity was not prolonged. When in 1905 Schlieffen, disabled by a kick from a horse, was absent from his post, Moltke acted for him, and the next year definitely succeeded him as Chief of the General Staff.

The names actually submitted, some time before, to the Kaiser as suitable had been those of Goltz and Beseler. Goltz, a famous military writer, and the prophet of the *Nation in Arms*, found, like many other soldiers, that active thought and the power of expressing it create uneasiness rather than appreciation in high places. Beseler, later the conqueror of Antwerp, belonged to the Engineers, and although Deputy Chief of the General Staff, was therefore ignored by the Kaiser, who "knew" only Guard and Cavalry officers. But, above all, the choice of Moltke seems to have been due to the Kaiser's belief in his historic name as an omen of victory. If Moltke's elevation was unjustified by his achievements, the strength of his pedestal enabled him to make a stand against interference from his "creator." He told the Kaiser frankly that at manœuvres "the decisions of the commanding generals are always influenced by the interference of Your Majesty, so that the officers lose all desire for initiative and become inert and unreliable." And the Kaiser gave way, abstaining from active command or interference, until July 1914. Moltke was thus emboldened to take liberties with the war plan of his illustrious predecessor. The first change was wise, politically at least. Moltke preferred the risk of delay by the forts of Liége rather than avoid them by crossing the strip of Dutch territory known as the Maastricht Appendix, an act of military convenience which might range Holland as well as Belgium on the side of Germany's foes. But Moltke revealed less moral audacity than his predecessor in matters that were purely military. Schlieffen had concentrated all his efforts on building up an overwhelming right wing in the projected advance into France. He had taken the calculated risk of weakening the left wing, with the view that this wing could retire gradually before a French onslaught without serious danger and by its very yielding draw the French on to their destruction by drawing them away from northwestern France, which would thus be all the more exposed to the smashing onrush of the German right wing.

Moltke shrank from the risk, and, as new reserves became available, strengthened the left wing at the expense of the right. And like many timid men, he wished to risk too little at the outset and to gain too much later, thinking that a strong left wing would not only avert initial danger but enable him to en-

velop the French armies on both flanks — repeating
1870 and leading to a greater Sedan. Thus, when
the test came, the German war machine was laboring
under too great a strain, and this, coupled with
Moltke's inability to keep control, caused the breakdown on the Marne and the loss of the first and
greatest chance of Germany's victory in the war.
Moltke's papers after his death threw a vivid light
not only on the complexity and rigidity of the German war machine, but on the way a national, as
opposed to a professional, army tends inevitably
toward war. Once set in motion, it gathers weight
and pace like an avalanche, escaping direction and
making almost hopeless any attempts either to orient
or to retard its course.

On July 31, 1914, Moltke was summoned by the
Kaiser and shown a telegram from the German
Ambassador in London which said that Secretary of
State Grey had informed him Great Britain would
engage to keep France out of the war, if Germany
would reciprocally engage not to undertake hostilities
against France. The Kaiser then said to Moltke:
"Now we need only wage war against Russia; thus
we simply march the whole of our army eastward."
Moltke replied: "Your Majesty, that is impossible.
The deployment of a host of millions of men cannot
be improvised; it means a whole year of laborious
work, and once settled, cannot be altered. If Your
Majesty insists on leading the whole army to the

East, it will not be an army ready for battle, but a disorderly crowd of unorganized armed men without supply arrangements."

The Kaiser was "much upset" and retorted bitterly: "Your uncle would have given me a different answer." The machine which they had created was beyond the power of men to control, and not only were they swept inevitably in its wake toward war, but they proved equally helpless to guide it strategically, once its ponderous and remorseless passage over the French frontier had begun.

Moltke, who had already disturbed the balance between the two wings which Schlieffen had contrived, upset it still more by repeated reductions in the weight of the marching right wing. He first detached active divisions to watch the fortresses of Antwerp, Givet, and Maubeuge, and then, on August 25, to reënforce the Eastern Front against Russia, in the belief that the decision in the West was already ensured! The delusion was strengthened by the roseate reports of the various army commanders, each anxious for his own credit, and by the failure of the Supreme Command to keep touch with — far less to keep control over — the advancing armies. A suspicion of the truth began to dawn upon Moltke through the comparatively small captures of men and guns, and in this state of doubt the Kaiser's easy optimism irritated him. "He has already a shout-hurrah mood that I hate like death." When disillusionment finally came in the Battle of the Marne, Moltke, more sensitive than his opponent, Joffre, lost his nerve. He felt instinctively that the loss of the Marne meant the ultimate loss of the war, and with still truer instinct remarked, "We shall have to pay for all that we have destroyed."

Between September 5 and 9 no orders from Moltke were issued to the Army Commands, and from September 7 to 9 no information or report as to the situation was sent by them to Moltke. These were the crucial days of the Marne battle, which began on September 6 and ended with the retreat of the German armies, beginning with the Second, on September 9! The fact would be incredible if it were not attested by ample evidence. This retreat was ordered rather than compelled, due to the panic fears of leaders so saturated with military convention that a slight indentation of their front and a partial bending of their flanks led them to conclude that, by the rules of the game, they were beaten. There was no necessity to fall back if they had appreciated the defensive power of modern arms as well as they appreciated the conventions of strategy. The French were unperturbed by the presence of the far deeper St. Mihiel wedge which remained in their front during four years, and in 1918 the Allied commanders did not find it necessary to fall back and straighten the line even when the enemy had driven wedges forty miles deep into their front. At the

Marne the German soldiers were not beaten, but only their leaders. On the morrow of this defeat Moltke was displaced, the failure of his physical vigor being made — according to customary subterfuge — the excuse for a dismissal really due to failure of moral vigor.

This sketch of Moltke, his character and career, is a necessary preliminary if we are to understand the problem of his successor, Falkenhayn, and the conditions which surrounded his advent to power. Moltke's confession on the eve of war that he could not alter the rigid plan had evidently both irritated the Kaiser and disturbed his confidence in Moltke's grip on the situation, for as early as August 10 the Chief of the Military Cabinet asked Falkenhayn privately if he was prepared to take over the duties of Chief of the General Staff. During the advance through Belgium into France, Falkenhayn had uneasy qualms over the blind and headlong pace of the German onrush, and urged the need and value of securing the advance by consolidating each step in its wake. On September 3 there is an entry in his diary: "Impressed again on Moltke . . . the necessity of occupying the north coast and also of halting for rest on the Marne." One of the most amazing features of the war is that the Germans, with the Allied armies in full retreat, made no attempt to secure the Channel ports, which lay at their mercy.

The British had evacuated Calais, Boulogne, and the whole coast as far as Le Havre, even transferred their base to St. Nazaire on the Bay of Biscay. German Uhlans roamed at will over the northwest of France, settled down in Amiens as if they were permanent lodgers, yet left the vital ports in tranquil isolation. A month later they were to sacrifice tens of thousands of lives in the vain attempt to gain what they could have secured without losing a drop of blood.

On the eve of the Battle of the Marne, September 5, there is this significant entry in Falkenhayn's diary : "The German Staff itself admits to-day that the retreat of the French is being carried out in complete order, but it cannot come to a new decision. . . . Only one thing is certain : our General Staff has completely lost its head. Schlieffen's notes do not help any further, and so Moltke's wits come to an end." A deadly sarcasm !

The choice of Falkenhayn to succeed Moltke was dictated not merely by Falkenhayn's record and the proved truth of his criticisms, but even more by his presence at General Headquarters as Minister of War. For the Germans had no wish to advertise the failure of their first chief, a confession that their plan had miscarried, and they could camouflage the change better by slipping Falkenhayn into Moltke's seat than by recalling anyone from the front. Moreover, although Falkenhayn took over the duties of Chief of the General Staff on September 14, his appointment was not publicly announced until November 3, and he retained the functions of Minister of War as well until February 1915.

The first need was to restore confidence and cohesion in an army defeated through no fault of its own. The rapidity of the recovery is a tribute both to the sound body of the army and to the tonic administered by Falkenhayn's reassertion of higher control. He had seen the faults of 1870 repeated, more disastrously, in 1914: the army commanders acting independently and taking their own course without attention to a Supreme Command which was wanting in the power to control them. Falkenhayn's fault here was that he swung too far to the other extreme, centralizing power excessively in his own person. His character and manner aggravated the failings of this tendency. If he was not well served, it was partly his own fault. The head of the Operations Section was a source of friction as well as a man of limited mind, but Falkenhayn, who realized Tappen's inadequacy, declared that he did not want an adviser, only a conscientious man who carried out his orders punctually. Aloof, reserved, notoriously ambitious, Falkenhayn was not the man to inspire affection in his subordinates or trust in his peers. General Stürgkh, Austrian representative at the German Headquarters, gives a vivid impression of him: "tall, slim, with a particularly youthful face, in which were

a pair of very sharp and clever but sarcastic eyes,
with the striking contrast of a very gray but very
thick head of hair."

Perhaps it was not surprising that under his régime
the commanders at the front emphasized their successes rather than their difficulties, a habit of facile
optimism which drew from him after one of his
visits the bitter comment that "the lies that these
Army Commanders combine in telling are quite
incredible." Sympathy is a better magnet for truth
than is sarcasm.

The reaction of the Marne on the two sides was
characteristic of the mentality and predisposition
of the rival commanders. The Allies, whose blind
optimism had led them into disaster after disaster
since the outset, were so elated — and inflated — by
the "miracle of the Marne" that they were carried
away by their ideas of a decisive manœuvre against
the German flank. In the "race to the sea" they
buoyantly made a series of inadequate and belated
attempts to turn the German flank, until they
suddenly came down with a bump, to find themselves
desperately, and almost despairingly, struggling to
hold out against the German onslaught at Ypres.

With the Central Powers the outlook of Falkenhayn was now the decisive influence, and the impression derived not merely from his critics but from his
own account is that neither the outlook nor the

direction was really clear as to its goal. He was too obsessed with the principle of security at the expense of the principle of concentration, and in his failure to fulfill the second he undermined the foundations of the first. On taking over the reins from Moltke, he still adhered to the Schlieffen plan of seeking a decision in the West, but the course he followed did not appear to have any far-reaching aim. Both in clearing his right rear by the reduction of Antwerp and in the subsequent effort to gain the Channel ports, Falkenhayn's guiding idea seems to have been merely that "of firmly establishing the right flank on the sea" as a protection to "the western territory of the Empire, with its sensitive as well as indispensable resources. . . ." His actions and his mental attitude were those of a commander striving to ward off impending defeat rather than one whose mighty army had only missed decisive victory by a hair's breadth. He erred on the side of pessimism as much as the Allies on the side of optimism. Nor, in pursuit of his limited object, did his method fulfill the Schlieffen principle of drawing from the left wing in order to mass on the vital right wing. The prolonged attacks in October and November around Ypres were made largely with raw formations, while war-experienced troops lay almost idle between the Aisne and the Vosges. Colonel Gröner, Director of the Field Railways, even went so far as to submit a detailed plan to Falkenhayn for the transfer of six army corps from the left to the right wing, but it was rejected. When we remember how close to the breaking point was the British line at Ypres, the verdict can only be that for a second time the German Supreme Command saved the Allies.

At this juncture, too, Ludendorff was pleading vehemently for reënforcements, to give weight to the wedge which he planned to drive into the joint of the Russian phalanx near Lodz. Without them, Ludendorff shattered the only serious advance during the war of the "Russian steam-roller" and almost surrounded a whole army. With them, the "almost" might have been deleted. But Falkenhayn missed the chance by delaying to send the reënforcements until failure in the long-drawn-out Ypres offensive had passed from assurance to fact.

Early in 1915 Falkenhayn, persuaded at last of the strength of the Allied trench-barrier, took the momentous decision to stand on the defensive in the West. But his object in so doing seems to have been vague. His feeling that the war must ultimately be decided in France led him to distrust the value, as he doubted the possibility, of a decision against Russia. Hence, while he realized that the Eastern Front was the only practicable theatre for operations in the near future, he withheld the necessary reënforcements until his hand was forced by the threatening situation of the Austro-Hungarian front. And even then he doled out reserves reluctantly and meagrely, enough to secure success, but never in the quantity and the time for decisive victory.

It is to his credit, however, that he realized a long war was now inevitable, and that he set to work to develop Germany's resources for such a war of attrition. The technique of field entrenchment was carried to a higher pitch than with any other country, the military railways were expanded for the lateral movement of reserves, the supply of munitions and of raw material for their manufacture was tackled so energetically and comprehensively that an ample flow was ensured from the spring of 1915 onward — a time when the British were only awakening to the problem. Here were laid the foundations of that economic organization and utilization of resources which were to be the secret of Germany's resisting power to the pressure of the British blockade.

The same period witnessed also the one great success for German diplomacy, the entry of Turkey into the war, although this was due fundamentally to a combination of pre-war causes with the course of events. Diplomacy finds its strongest arguments in military success. And it received strong support from Falkenhayn, who was convinced of "the decisive importance of Turkey joining in the struggle," first, as a barrier against the channel of Allied munition supply to Russia, and secondly, as a distraction of the military efforts of Britain and Russia.

At the same time a vast campaign of propaganda was launched in Asia, to undermine British prestige and the loyalty of Britain's Mohammedan subjects. The defect of German propaganda, its crudeness, was less apparent when directed to primitive races than when applied to the civilized peoples of Europe and America.

But while Falkenhayn was expanding the basis of Germany's war efforts he was nearly unseated himself. · Moltke, since his fall, had been intriguing for Falkenhayn's removal and his own return, on the grounds that Falkenhayn was too young and did not inspire confidence in the army. The failure at Ypres reënforced this attempt, which apparently was supported by the Kaiserin and Hindenburg; but Falkenhayn, with equal craft, checkmated it by telling the Kaiser that Moltke's own physician had reported him unfit. The tale served its purpose, and Falkenhayn remained.

On the Eastern Front, the campaign of 1914 had shown that a German force could count upon defeating any larger Russian force, but that when Austrians and Russians met on an equality victory rested with the Russians.

From the beginning of 1915 the Russians developed a steadily increasing pressure on the Austro-Hungarian front in the Carpathians, threatening to force the mountain gateways into the Hungarian plain. Falkenhayn was driven, reluctantly, to dispatch

German reënforcements as a stiffening to the Austrians, and thus was dragged into a relief offensive in the East rather than adopting it as a clearly defined plan. In contrast, Ludendorff, who was the directing brain of the German forces in the East, had his eyes firmly fixed on the ultimate object, and from now on advocated unceasingly a whole-hearted effort to break Russia. He differed from Falkenhayn, not merely over the object but over the plan, urging instead of a direct blow at the Russian forces in the Polish salient a wide Napoleonic manœuvre through Vilna, to cut their communications. Ludendorff's was a strategy of decision, Falkenhayn's at best a strategy of attrition.

Nor was this the only mental tug of wills, for Falkenhayn was throughout in ceaseless dispute with Conrad von Hötzendorf, the Chief of the Austrian General Staff. Conrad had launched the Austrian army in a premature and costly offensive into Poland, August 1914, to relieve the Russian pressure on Germany, while the latter was seeking a decision in France, and now he considered that Austria should be given full support in repayment for this sacrifice. Withheld until the Austrian resistance was severely strained, the growing danger of his ally's collapse forced Falkenhayn to concede support, if not in generous measure.

On April 1, 1915, Conrad proposed to Falkenhayn a plan to get the most advantage from these slender reënforcements — a rupture of the Russian left centre between the Carpathians and the Upper Vistula. This Tarnow-Gorlice sector offered the least obstacles to an advance and the best protection to the flanks of a penetration. Falkenhayn accepted the proposal. By suppressing the earlier correspondence and quoting only his own letter of the thirteenth, he tried to give the impression in his post-war book that he originated the plan. To satisfy the prestige of both allies, the combined Austro-German attacking force was put under a German general, Mackensen, and he in turn under the Austrian Supreme Command.

A large cavalry raid from East Prussia in the north and the gas attack at Ypres — thus disclosing prematurely for a trifling advantage this new means of surprise — were used to cloak the concentration, between Tarnow and Gorlice, of seven German and seven Austrian divisions and 1500 guns against a front weakly held — by only six Russian divisions — and lacking in rear lines of trenches.

On May 2, 1915, after an intense bombardment had flattened the Russian trenches, the attack was launched and swept through with little opposition. The surprise was complete, the exploitation rapid, and the whole Russian line along the Carpathians was rolled up, until on May 14 the advance through Galicia reached the San, eighty miles from its starting point. Defeat almost turned into disaster when this river was forced at Jaroslav, but the impetus of the advance had momentarily spent itself and German reserves were lacking. Falkenhayn now realized that he had committed himself too far in Galicia to draw back, and that only by bringing more troops from France could he hope to fulfill his purpose of transferring troops back there — as this could only be possible when Russia's offensive power was crippled and her menace to Austria removed.

A fresh bound captured Lemburg by June 22, but the Russians, from their vast man-power resources, had almost made good the loss of 400,000 prisoners, and Falkenhayn's anxiety about the stability of his troops drew him on willy-nilly to continue the offensive, although still with limited objects and with one eye on the situation in France. He now changed the direction from eastward to northward and in conjunction ordered Ludendorff — all this time fretting impatiently in East Prussia — to strike southeastward. Ludendorff argued that this plan was too much of a frontal attack, and that although the closing in of the two wings might squeeze the Russians, it would not cut off their retreat. He wanted to strike far back at their communications while they were still entangled in Poland, but Falkenhayn again rejected the plan, fearing that it would mean a deeper German commitment. The upshot proved Ludendorff's forecast, and at the end of September the Russian retreat, after a nerve-

racking series of escapes from the salients which
the Germans since May had systematically created
and then sought to pinch out, came to a definite
halt on a straightened line from Riga on the Baltic
to Czernowitz on the Rumanian frontier. Russia
had been badly lamed, but not destroyed, and although never again a direct menace to Germany, she
was to keep Austria on the rack and to delay the full
concentration of German strength in the West for
two years, until 1918.

Late in August Falkenhayn decided to break off
large-scale operations on the Eastern Front in order
to fulfill and extend his policy of security at all
points. Bulgaria's entry into the war was now
arranged and he wished to exploit it in order to remove finally the menace from Serbia, and to open
direct railway communication with his easternmost
ally, Turkey, which was still hard-pressed at the
Dardanelles. Further, he wished to transfer troops
back to France to meet the Franco-British offensive
expected in September.

Beginning on October 6, the converging attack of
the Austro-German and Bulgarian armies overran
Serbia and drove the remnant of her armies out of the
country, despite a belated and inadequate attempt
of her allies to go to her succor. The French and
British forces barely saved themselves by a hasty
retreat to Salonika, to which they held on for reasons
primarily of policy and prestige. Thither the Ser-

bian army was shipped, to be reconstituted for a
fresh share in the struggle. Falkenhayn was satis-
fied to have opened direct communication with
Turkey and opposed Conrad's wish for a continuation of the offensive in order to drive the Franco-
British forces from their foothold at Salonika. In
his book he puts forward the excuse that examination
of the railway system showed that it was insufficient
to supply the needs of such an offensive; but recent
documents have revealed that the head of the Railway Section, who was sent to investigate, actually
reported the opposite.

His limited object achieved, Falkenhayn preferred
to leave Salonika in passivity, under guard of the
Bulgarians, while he steadily withdrew the German
forces for use elsewhere. With gentle sarcasm the
Germans termed Salonika their "largest internment
camp," and with half a million Allied troops locked
up there the jibe had some justification — until
1918. Then the enemy foothold which Falkenhayn
had ignored was suddenly expanded, and the collapse
of Bulgaria knocked away the first prop of the Germanic Alliance.

With the dawn of 1916 Falkenhayn, feeling now
secure everywhere, prepared to fulfill his long-
cherished plan for an offensive in the West, but with
characteristic limitations. Always an adherent of
the strategy of attrition, he now carried this ruling
idea into tactics, and produced the new form of

attack by methodical stages, each with a limited objective.

In a memorandum to the Kaiser at Christmas 1915 he argued that England was the staple of the enemy alliance. "The history of the English wars against the Netherlands, Spain, France, and Napoleon is being repeated. Germany can expect no mercy from this enemy, so long as he still retains the slightest hope of achieving his object." Except by submarine warfare, however, England and her army were out of reach, for Falkenhayn considered that the English sector of the front did not lend itself to offensive operations. "In view of our feelings for our arch-enemy in the war that is certainly distressing, but it can be endured if we realize that for England the campaign on the Continent . . . is at bottom a side show. Her real weapons here are the French, Russian, and Italian armies." Falkenhayn regarded Russia as already paralyzed and Italy's military achievements as unlikely to affect the situation. "Only France remains." "France has almost arrived at the end of her military effort. If her people can be made to understand clearly that in a military sense they have nothing more to hope for, the breaking-point would be reached and England's best weapon knocked out of her hand."

He added that a break-through in mass was unnecessary, and that instead the Germans should aim to bleed France to death by choosing a point of attack "for the retention of which the French would be compelled to throw in every man they have." Such objectives were either Belfort or Verdun, and Falkenhayn chose Verdun, because it was a menace to the main German communications, because it offered a salient and so cramped the defenders, and because of the moral effect if so renowned a place were lost to France.

Once again Conrad disagreed with Falkenhayn, preferring a concentrated blow to knock Italy out of the war, and arguing that a decision there was more feasible than in the French alternative. Nor was he the only dissentient. The German Crown Prince, who was to have the honor of commanding the Verdun attack, felt that attrition was a two-edged weapon, and thought that it would be wiser to finish with Russia first.

Both were overruled, and the Verdun "blood-letting" incisions began on February 21.

The keynote of the tactical plan was a continuous series of limited advances which by their menace should draw the French reserves into the mincing-machine of the German artillery. And each of these advances was itself to be secured from loss by an intense artillery bombardment, brief for surprise and compensating its short duration by the number of batteries and their rapidity of fire. By this means the objective would be taken and consolidated before the defenders could move up their reserves for counterattack.

But the theory of limitation was carried to an extreme — the first day the front of attack was only two and a half miles. Thus the few scattered packets of surviving Frenchmen caused more delay than would have been possible on a frontage of rational width. This idea of punching a narrow hole was contrary to the advice of members of Falkenhayn's own staff and the executive commanders. When the front was at last extended on March 6 to the other bank of the Meuse, the chance of a break-through had faded, for the French had recovered from their surprise and repaired their original negligence, and the numbers were now balanced. Even so, the superior technique of the German troops and the reluctance of the French to cede a yard of ground — Falkenhayn had at least gauged the French temperament correctly — turned the balance of attrition in favor of the Germans. But the slow and costly process and the absence of tangible result brought no credit to Falkenhayn's "limited" strategy, and the discontent rose to a height when the offensive failed to prevent ripostes elsewhere. For on June 5, 1916, the Russian army, which Falkenhayn had thought that he could disregard, came to the rescue of France. Under the slight pressure of Brusilov's impromptu advance, the Austrian front collapsed and within three days Brusilov had taken 200,000 prisoners.

Never has a mere demonstration had so amazing a success since the walls of Jericho fell at Joshua's trumpet blasts. Although soon checked by its own lack of weight and by prompt German intervention, it compelled Falkenhayn to withdraw troops from the Western Front, and so abandon his plan for a counterstroke against the British offensive preparing on the Somme, as well as the hope of nourishing his Verdun attrition process. It led Rumania to take her fateful decision to enter the war on the side of the Entente. And it caused the downfall of Falkenhayn and his replacement in the Supreme Command by Hindenburg and Ludendorff. For although Rumania's unexpected entry was the ostensible reason, the underlying one was the fact that Falkenhayn's "limited" strategy in 1915 had made possible the Russian recovery which stultified the plan of 1916. Falkenhayn's strategy was history's latest example of the folly of half measures.

He was offered as consolation the post of Ambassador at Constantinople and after declining this was given executive command of the Ninth Army for the campaign against Rumania. Here, if a difficult subordinate, he regilded his laurels by conducting the offensive which threw the Rumanians out of Transylvania, broke through the Carpathians just before the winter snows, and captured Bucharest through a convergent manœuvre with Mackensen's forces from the south. Later he was sent to Turkey

for the purpose of regaining Mesopotamia from the
British, and when this scheme was abandoned, owing
to the burning of the depots with all the ammunition
for the campaign, he took over the command in
Palestine. He arrived in Jerusalem the day after
Allenby's attack on Beersheba, which had forestalled
his own offensive, and in a vain attempt to stay the
British advance he dissipated the scanty Turkish
resources in a series of petty counterattacks. His
misunderstanding of local conditions and of the
psychology of Turkish troops helped to complete
the bankruptcy of Turkish man-power, but early in
1918, before the final disaster, he gave way to Liman
von Sanders.

Before his death in 1922 he had issued his own
account of his work in the Supreme Command and
in Rumania, and the studiously impersonal tone —
cloaking omissions which cleverly distorted the facts
— combined with the likeness of his "limited"
strategy to their own to win him undue credit among
British military leaders. Thus the pernicious legend
has been created, by those who do not trouble to
delve beneath the surface, that Falkenhayn was "the
most competent and most far-seeing of the German
commanders and strategists."

His countrymen, who knew him intimately, knew
him better. Colonel Bauer, the one "fixture" in the
headquarters of the Supreme Command throughout

the war, and the invaluable assistant in turn of
Moltke, Falkenhayn, and Ludendorff, has said of
Falkenhayn that he possessed nearly every gift of
nature "except the intuition of a commander; his
decisions were half measures and he wavered even
over these. He would probably have made a great
statesman, diplomat, or parliamentarian, and was
least of all qualified to command in the field."

The antithesis of Foch, Falkenhayn was an uncompromising realist, and the very excess of this valuable
quality was his own poison. Like Napoleon's opponents, he saw "too many things at once," and, above
all, saw the enemy's strength too clearly. His realization that England was the soul and will of the
hostile alliance was proof of his insight, but it merely
depressed him.

Falkenhayn's course might well serve as an object
lesson of Napoleon's warning against the "worst
course, which almost always in war is the most
pusillanimous — or, if you will, the most prudent."
He was the ablest and most scientific general,
"penny wise, pound foolish," who ever ruined his
country by a refusal to take calculated risks. Limitation of risks led to liquidation.

MARSHAL GALLIENI
THE REAL VICTOR OF THE MARNE

MARSHAL GALLIENI

THE REAL VICTOR OF THE MARNE

FIVE years after his death, the shade of Joseph Simon Gallieni received the posthumous honor of being created Marshal of France. It was a belated but sincere recognition from the French Government that in the dark days of early September, 1914, he had saved France, and had changed the face of the World War by bringing about the "miracle of the Marne." For years the truth was concealed by public ignorance, superficial assumptions, and the jealous dignity of a superior and his entourage, who needed to borrow the laurels of victory in order to cover the shame of earlier disasters. Moreover, even among the governmental leaders who knew or surmised the facts, it was thought necessary to maintain the fiction in order to sustain the spirit of France and the confidence of her allies, for to the outside world the Generalissimo — Joffre — was the symbol of France triumphant. To-day, when this need has passed with the emergency, justice and gratitude demand that the world should recognize Gallieni, rather than Joffre, as the victor of the Marne.

Joseph Simon Gallieni was born on April 24, 1849, at St. Béat on the skirts of the Pyrenees — yet

another of the famous soldiers of France who have
sprung from that mountain region. And, if heredi-
tary environment had an influence on his military
qualities, there was an extra significance in the fact
that his family was Corsican in origin and with a
military tradition.

Entering St. Cyr when he was nineteen, he passed
out, to a commission in the marine infantry (colonial
service troops), on July 15, 1870 — the day of the
declaration of war against Germany. This early and
bitter experience of war was for most French officers
to be followed by forty years of peace soldiering, but
not so with Gallieni. The service he had chosen
cast his lot in foreign climes and, through a series
of colonial campaigns, paved his way to a mission
of colonization; for, unlike most of his famous
comrades and compatriots, Gallieni would have
had a niche in history if a European war had
never come again within his lifetime. In the late
seventies, as explorer and soldier, he played an
important rôle in extending and establishing French
influence in the region of the upper Niger, and
after a spell in Martinique, returned again to
West Africa to become governor of Upper Senegal.
An acute observer and a scientific mind, his work
and writings rendered almost as much service to
geographical research as to France. In 1893 he
traveled east across the Indian Ocean to command
a military district in Tongking and secure the

© *Keystone View Co.*

GALLIENI

C.O.D.
Counting on Piano

French hold on the country. Three years later he was called back to a still greater rôle as governor-general and commander in chief of the new French colony of Madagascar.

Madagascar was in revolt, owing to the weakness of his predecessor. Gallieni not only crushed the revolt and completed the full subjugation of the island, but by his political measures and development of the island's economic resources left it peaceful and prosperous. Henceforth Madagascar was to be as closely associated with the name of Gallieni as Morocco later with the name of Lyautey. And like another great colonial administrator in Africa, Kitchener, Gallieni was to be called to the rescue of his motherland in the hour of supreme peril. But if the outcome was in part to dim as well as to extend Kitchener's wider fame, Gallieni's niche in the hall of fame was to be enlarged during his life and still more after his death. History has few stranger coincidences than the parallel course of the careers of these two great soldiers. Both were launched into active service in the same year and the same war, — the War of 1870 against Germany, — both carved their fortunes in Africa, both became famous colonial rulers. And they died within ten days of each other, both self-sacrificed on the altar of duty in a war against the same foe they had faced together as boys.

Recalled from Madagascar in 1905, Gallieni became military governor of Lyon and commander of the 14th Army Corps. After so many years in colonial expeditions and administration he had lost touch with the higher study of war and, accustomed to dealing with isolated packets of men in bush and desert fighting, found difficulty in imitating the facile mastery of those who gayly manœuvred armies of millions on paper maps. Like Joffre, he was out of his depth; but, whereas Joffre had been building fortifications, Gallieni had been building men, and, while Joffre drifted with the current, Gallieni's quicker intelligence enabled him to strike out for a point where he could gain a firm footing. This point was the practical training of the troops. He did not attempt to lay down the law on strategical questions. Indeed, he was modest enough to realize his own handicaps and to say to his predecessor on arrival, "I have come from the tropics: I don't know in the least what has been happening at home. Let me have a young Staff College graduate to give me lessons." And the hero of Senegal, Tongking, and Madagascar sat humbly at the feet of this Captain Galonnier. Even when he had gained sufficient confidence to direct schemes and large-scale exercises, he hesitated to be dogmatic in exposition, and so hardly impressed his true powers upon his hearers until he was confronted by a real instead of a hypothetical enemy.

He was still learning when the crisis in the French Command developed in 1911. The reason that led

Gallieni to throw the weight of his name and influence in the scales against Michel, the commander in chief designate, was probably less that he distrusted Michel's strategical policy than that he was disquieted by Michel's personality. Another factor may have been that his belief in the value of training led him to have little faith in Michel's project of utilizing masses of reservists. But strategically we shall see Gallieni, shortly after, taking the same view as Michel of the likelihood of a German advance through Belgium. When Michel, thrown down by all his colleagues on the Conseil Supérieur de la Guerre, was forced to resign, Gallieni could have had the succession to his place. Gallieni's scruples forbade him to reap a personal advantage by his opposition and he declined the prize, on the excuse of his age and the limitation of his experience to colonial warfare. Messimy, the Minister of War, asked him to take two days for reflection. But Gallieni was still firm, saying, "It is my duty to repeat that you have a great and cruel duty to perform — that of removing General Michel; but I, who have indicted him in front of you, cannot accept to be substituted for him." In the impasse, Messimy asked him for alternative names. Gallieni suggested first Pau, a deeply read and intellectually qualified soldier, but politically suspect for his clerical views; secondly, Joffre, who had served under him in Madagascar; and the Minister of War accepted the latter suggestion.

Gallieni's recommendation of his former subordinate was the one disservice he rendered to France and the worst to himself. He certainly did not realize that he was merely creating a massive puppet which would dance to the measure dictated by the "Young Turks" of the General Staff, for he was by no means filled with their blind faith in a victory march to the tune of the *offensive à outrance*. In 1912 he insisted that war ought to be avoided, as the French army was unready, and in March 1914 he directed a war game at the Centre of Higher Military Studies which foreshadowed the march of the German armies through Belgium. The danger so impressed him that in his report he urged that Dunkerque, Lille, and Maubeuge ought to be put in a state to act as breakwaters to the German tide, and that a field army should also be disposed on this flank. His warning fell on the deaf ears of leaders who were confident that they had only to advance to conquer, and that it was waste of effort to renovate fortresses in their rear. A month later he reached the age for retirement, and although, in tribute to his prestige and work, he was nominally retained on the active list, he settled down in peaceful repose on a little estate at St. Raphaël. His contentment was soon doubly shattered. For, while the Austrian guns were sounding the tocsin of war on the Danube facing Belgrade, Gallieni was standing by the grave-side of his wife.

From his private sorrows and the débris of his dream of a tranquil eveningtide to his life, a telegram from the Minister of War came to rescue him. Dated July 31, it notified him that in case of mobilization he would be deputy to the commander in chief, Joffre, and his successor, if the need arose. But when he arrived in Paris he was left to kick his heels in impatient idleness, for Joffre showed no desire to have a potential successor at his side or to keep Gallieni *au courant* with the operations of which he might be called on to take charge. The Minister of War asked Joffre to attach Gallieni to his headquarters, but was refused. As a courtesy a room in the Ministry of War was given to Gallieni, and there he sat studying maps and such bare information as Joffre chose to send to the Ministry. All Gallieni could do was to utter unheeded warnings against the idea that the German halt at Liége was a serious check, against premature rejoicings over the early superficial success of the Belgian resistance, against any attempt to push forward into Belgium — and the German noose.

On August 15 the Minister, disquieted, sent Gallieni to discuss the situation with Joffre, who merely spoke to Gallieni for a moment in an antechamber and then left him to a staff officer. Five days later alarming telegrams began to flow in from Joffre's headquarters, and when Joffre admitted the collapse of his rash hopes the Government, panic-stricken, was minded to throw over the commander in chief.

A lesser man than Gallieni would have exploited this crisis, for Joffre's dismissal meant Gallieni's succession, but instead he joined with the Minister of War in dissuading the Cabinet from swapping horses when actually in midstream.

The defense of the capital was a different question, and on August 26 Gallieni was named the military governor of Paris — when the enemy were almost at its gates. As he remarked, "They have given me a formidable task. Nothing is ready and the minutes are centuries." Having done the best it could for the menaced capital, the Government departed hastily for Bordeaux, leaving Gallieni to issue the famous proclamation, inspiring, yet with an undercurrent of sarcasm: "Army of Paris, Inhabitants of Paris, the members of the Government of the Republic have left Paris in order to give a new impulse to the national defense. I have received a mandate to defend Paris against the invader. This mandate I shall carry out to the end." The sarcasm was justified and explained by his private comment: "The Government has left for Bordeaux and left me alone in the presence of a population which have been deceived until now by lying communiqués." And it was significant of a fine sentiment that Gallieni, before accepting this charge to defend the capital, asked if its meaning was fully realized, that it might involve the destruction of historic buildings and works of art which are the glory of Paris.

His task of defense appeared to him, as he said, to comprise three elements — military defense, moral defense, and supply. While he pressed on the work of throwing up trenches and obstacles, pacified the fearful, and suppressed the alarmists, he showed an unusually acute appreciation of the reaction of the three elements of security upon each other. From experience of the 1870 siege he had culled the subtle lesson that in order to spread confidence — confidence particularly in the foresight of their leaders — "it was not only necessary that Paris should not want for bread, but that it should eat the same bread." To this end he kept a firm hand on the wholesalers and retailers, checked profiteering, supervised distribution, and, as another moral safeguard, started a campaign against drunkenness and the opportunity for it.

This concern with the internal conditions and immediate defense of Paris did not prevent him keeping his eyes on a wider horizon. Thus, by exceeding his duty, he perceived and seized the chance to save not merely Paris but France. On August 25, when he had been warned to take over the military governorship, he had told the Minister of War, Messimy, that it was essential, for the defense of Paris, unprepared for resistance, to have a mobile force of at least three army corps beyond the actual garrison. The Minister telegraphed an order, accordingly, to Joffre; Gallieni wired direct; nothing happened. Two days later there was a reconstruction of the Government and Messimy was replaced by Millerand, to whom Gallieni renewed his urgent pleas. All that Joffre could offer, in response to repeated telegrams, was the statement: "The German army will not be before Paris for some days," — it was already within gunshot of the outposts, — "Maunoury's army and the territorial troops of the entrenched camp ought to suffice to defend Paris." Maunoury's army was the force which Joffre had hastily assembled near Amiens for an imagined return to the offensive, only for it to be engulfed in the ebbing tide of the Allied armies. Swept back in the general retreat, its course brought it to shelter within the entrenched zone of Paris, and, as it was separated from the main armies, Joffre had no option but to leave it in Gallieni's hands — a welcome reënforcement, if not all that he had asked for. And the very fact of relinquishing direct control of this force, which had been intended for a counterstroke, appears one of the numerous proofs that Joffre had also relinquished any idea of an early return to the offensive.

On September 1, Joffre issued an order for the retreat of the Allied armies to be continued to a line south of the Seine, Aube, and Ornain rivers. Not only was the effect of this to take the armies away from and far to the southeast of Paris, but a commander who is contemplating an early counteroffensive does not place the obstacle of a river barrier between himself and the enemy. And a further note to the army commanders next day added that it was Joffre's intention to "organize and fortify" this line, whence he planned to deliver not an immediate but an ultimate counteroffensive. That same day he replied to a suggestion of a stand on the Marne, made by Sir John French and communicated through the Minister of War, "I do not believe it possible to envisage a general action on the Marne with the whole of our forces. But I consider that the coöperation of the English army in the defense of Paris is the only course that can give an advantageous result." To the Minister of War and Gallieni he repeated the same verdict.

This array of evidence is more than sufficient to dispel the legend that Joffre had any preconceived intention of giving battle on the Marne or that he planned the counterstroke which wrenched victory from disaster. But in the evening of September 3 an insignificant action elsewhere was to have momentous consequences. An aviator flying over the area where the German columns were advancing remarked signs of a change of direction. This was reported to Gallieni, who ordered for the next morning fresh reconnaissances by aircraft and cavalry. These confirmed the fact that the German columns, instead of continuing their march south toward Paris, were wheeling southeast past the outskirts of the entrenched camp. Shut up in his office, Gallieni spent an hour in study of the map and in reflection. Then, his plan formed, he ordered Maunoury's army to get ready to move eastward for a blow against the Germans' flank, and informed Joffre by telephone of his own preparatory moves, urging the Commander in Chief to consent to a counteroffensive. This consent was necessary, not only to ensure a combined effort, but because Joffre had persuaded the new Minister of War to subordinate Gallieni to himself.

Gallieni's inspired initiative, however, made an impression but no more on the slow-thinking Commander in Chief. That was not surprising. Four days before, a staff officer with the Fifth Army, Captain Fagalde, had found in the wallet of a dead German officer the German order for a change of direction, and sent it to G. Q. G. on the morning of September 2. Yet even this vital piece of information, earlier and more definite than any Gallieni gleaned, had evoked no active response from Joffre, although confirmed by British air reports which had been communicated to G. Q. G. on September 3. To save time while Joffre was making up his mind, Gallieni rushed off by motor to Melun to explain the new situation to the British, and if possible gain their coöperation. Unhappily, Sir John French was absent from his headquarters, and at first Gallieni could not even find the Chief of Staff. It was a curious scene. Gallieni, on his side, found the British staff unsettled and depressed, not hesitating to say that if England had known the situation of the French army she would certainly not have entered the war. They, on their side, were hardly in the mood to discern the underlying qualities of this most unmilitary-looking military genius, bespectacled and untidy, with shaggy moustache, black buttoned boots, and yellow leggings. Little wonder, perhaps, that one eminent soldier with a pungent gift of humor remarked that "no British officer would be seen speaking to such a — comedian."

Gallieni pointed out to the Chief of Staff that it was vital to seize the opportunity which the Germans had given by offering their right flank; told him that the "Army of Paris" was already in motion against the German flank, and begged that the British should cease to retreat and join with his forces in an offensive next day. The British Chief of Staff showed "une grande répugnance . . . à entrer dans nos vues," and declared that he could do nothing in the absence of his Commander. After waiting three hours in vain for Sir John French's return, Gallieni had to leave with no more than the promise of a telephone message later. This brought no satisfaction, for its purport was that the British would continue their retreat next day. Their decision had been confirmed by receiving a letter, written that morning, from Joffre, who said, "My intention, in the present situation, is to pursue the execution of the plans that I have had the honor to communicate

to you — that of retiring behind the Seine — and
only to engage on the selected line with all forces
united." The meagre influence which the news of
the enemy's change of direction had achieved was
shown by a subsequent paragraph, which said, "In
the case of the German armies continuing their movement toward the S-S-W . . . perhaps you will agree
that your action can be most effectively applied on
the right bank of this river, between the Marne and
Seine." This casual qualification to the definite
opening statement gave the British little encourage-
ment to fall in with Gallieni's audacious suggestion.
There is a dramatic contrast between the sluggish
working of Joffre's mind, gradually but all too slowly
veering round, and Gallieni's swift *coup d'œil* and
instantaneous reaction.

Yet, if Gallieni's *coup d'œil* gained the opportunity, it was, as he himself said, "*coups de téléphone*
which gained the Battle of the Marne." For on
returning to his headquarters in Paris he had found
a belated message from Joffre which was favorable
to his proposal for a counterstroke, but preferred it
to be delivered south of the Marne — where it would
have lost the greater effect given by a blow against
the enemy's flanks and rear.

Gallieni seized the telephone, got through to Joffre,
and by the fervor and force of his arguments at last
won his sanction for the Army of Paris to strike north
of the Marne as part of a general counteroffensive by

the left-wing armies.[1]   Joffre promised to obtain the
coöperation of the British.   Gallieni promptly issued
orders (10.30 P.M.) to Maunoury's army, which he
reënforced, and a few hours later Joffre's telegraphic
orders for the general offensive arrived, fixing the
date for the sixth of September — it was too late now
for the fifth.   The delay had worse consequences.
Next morning, while Maunoury's troops were moving east toward the enemy, the British were marching leisurely south — away from their enemy — in
accordance with their original orders.   When they
turned about on the sixth, they had much ground to
recover, and were not as quick in retracing their
steps as the situation demanded.   This lack of
pressure enabled Kluck, commanding the German

[1] After Gallieni's morning message, Joffre had been moved so far as to send
a telegram, timed 12.45 P.M., to Franchet d'Espérey (Fifth Army) inquiring "if
he thought that his troops were in a state to take the offensive with chance of
success" — an inquiry which showed no suggestion of either keenness or urgency
of action.   At 4 P.M. Franchet d'Espérey, after discussion with Henry Wilson,
sub-chief of the British General Staff, sent a reply which said that "the battle
cannot take place before the day after to-morrow," and that he would continue
his retreat on the 5th, attacking on the 6th.   At 4.45 P.M. he sent a qualifying
note, even less encouraging.   "In order that the operation may be successful
the necessary conditions are (1) the close and absolute coöperation of the Sixth
Army debouching on the left bank of the Ourcq . . . on the morning of the
sixth.   It must reach the Ourcq to-morrow . . . or the British won't budge.
(2) My army can fight on the 6th but its situation is not brilliant.   No reliance
can be placed on the Reserve divisions."   What was likely to be the effect on a
Joffre of such a discouraging reply to his tentative inquiry?   To strengthen his
hesitation.   Little wonder that Gallieni had to call on all his powers of argument
when telephoning late that night.   If any doubt remained that this *coup de
téléphone* was the decisive factor it would be dispelled by the fact that Joffre's
orders for the counteroffensive were only sent out a little before midnight —
after this telephone argument.

flank army — the First — to leave only a cavalry
screen facing the British and to pull back the two
army corps from this sector to reënforce the one hard-
pressed army corps which was trying to hold off
Maunoury's menacing advance against the German
rear. The arrival of these fresh forces began to
check Maunoury's advance on the seventh, and
Gallieni pushed forward every possible reserve he
could scrape up in order to strengthen Maunoury.

Here occurred the immortal episode of the Paris
taxicabs. The Seventh Division had just detrained
in Paris, but it was forty miles from the battle front.
If it marched thither it would be too late, and there
was insufficient rail transport to take the whole
of the division. That afternoon the police held up
taxicabs in the streets, bundled the passengers out,
and, after collecting six hundred cabs, filled them with
soldiers. During the night this forerunner of the
future motorized column swept, as only Paris taxicabs can sweep, through the suburbs and past their
amazed inhabitants, making two journeys, and next
morning the whole division was concentrated on the
battlefield.

The pressure on the Germans gained extra force
from the fact that it was directed against the enemy's
rear flank. If Gallieni had received the two further
army corps for which he had asked days before, and
which were only just arriving piecemeal, the German
forces south of the Marne might well have been cut

off and the battle been as decisive tactically as it was strategically. Even in the actual situation the menace was such that Kluck called back his two remaining army corps, thus creating a twenty-mile-wide gap between him and the neighboring army of Bülow. The consequences were fatal. Although Kluck was able to hold and even press back Maunoury's troops, the gap in the southern front gave Franchet d'Espérey's army the chance to menace Bülow's exposed flank; and when, on top of this, news came that the British, who lay between Maunoury and Franchet d'Espérey, were advancing into the centre of the gap, it was the signal for the German retreat, which began on September 9. If the continuance of the British withdrawal on September 5 had marred the chance of a crushing victory, it was a pleasant irony of fate that their very withdrawal made possible the victory as actually achieved.

This victory might have been more decisive — to the shortening of the war — if its creator had not been removed from control at the beginning of the pursuit. For on September 11 Joffre informed Gallieni that he would resume direct control of Maunoury's army, leaving Gallieni to fret his soul within the confines of Paris while watching the fruits of victory slipping from the grasp of his slow-thinking superior. Throughout the battle Gallieni's governing idea had been to direct all reserves to the north, toward the enemy's rear, although several times frustrated by Joffre. With Gallieni's disappearance the advance became purely frontal, giving the Germans the breathing space to reorganize and stand firm on the line of the Aisne. Not until then did Joffre's slow mind awake to the idea of concentrating by rail a fresh *mass of manœuvre* behind the German flank. As a result, in the so-called "race to the sea," the Allies were always "twenty-four hours and an army corps late," until the trench front stretched to the sea, with ten fair provinces of France locked in on the German side.

The question has often been posed whether the trench stalemate would have come to pass if France had possessed a Napoleon. Although the unappreciated defensive power of modern weapons and the unwieldy masses of 1914 weighted the scales against the mobility and decisiveness of warfare, the Gallieni interlude raises a doubt. For not only did Gallieni afford the one instance of "Napoleonic *coup d'œil*" witnessed on the Western Front in 1914–1918, but his intuition, his boldness of manœuvre, and his swift decision were so vivid a contrast to that of the other leaders, French, British, and German, as to suggest that it was possible to snatch a decision by manœuvre from the jaws of trench warfare, before the artisan swallowed the artist.

The hypothesis is strengthened by the fact that Gallieni's influence was exercised under the most shackling conditions. The command of a fortress was governed by rules and limitations which ordained a strictly defensive rôle, even gave the governor power to refuse assistance to the field armies, and discouraged him from any wider horizon than that of his immediate responsibility for the defense of the fortress. It was the irony of fortune that the commander in chief in the field should have led the way to universal siege warfare, that the commander of a fortress should have conceived and launched the most decisive manœuvre of the war. Yet war is a game where the joker counts, and when Joffre withheld the trump Gallieni played the joker. As he remarked later, half humorously, half bitterly, "There has not been a Battle of the Marne. Joffre's instructions ordained a retreat on the Seine and the evacuation of Verdun and of Nancy. Sarrail did not obey: he saved Verdun. De Castelnau held on to the Grande Couronné: he saved Nancy. I have taken the offensive. As for asserting now that it is the Commander in Chief — who had gone back far to the rear while I advanced — who conducted, foresaw, and arranged it all . . . it is hard to believe!"

For, from the moment that the Battle of the Marne was waged and won in spite of his original intentions, Joffre's satellites industriously propagated the legend that the battle was the fruit of a masterly and foreordained strategic plan, and Joffre himself showed no inclination to discourage the legend or reject the stolen laurels. Yet he had been eager to divest himself of blame if failure had been the result. At the opening of the battle he had telegraphed to the President of the Republic and the Premier: "General Gallieni having attacked prematurely," — later revelations have shown that even a day's delay would have meant the collapse of the French centre, — "the Commander in Chief has given the order to suspend the retreat and return to the offensive."

Gallieni waited in vain for further scope now that the tide of battle had rolled back from Paris. The neglect caused wide comment and a visitor to Joffre was bold enough to mention it. Joffre's noncommittal reply was: "He is difficult to place, but if he waits he will probably be given an important post." Joffre's idea of this was to offer Gallieni the succession to Maunoury, his subordinate of the Marne. This was well calculated to provoke the refusal that it met. At last the Government proposed to give Gallieni the command of a group of armies, but Joffre refused.

What made Gallieni's enforced passivity more trying was his conviction of the futility of the Allied strategy. As early as October 1914, on returning from a visit to the front, he remarked: "We shall not break through; we shall not make a gap. Joffre is too content to be in trenches." A year later, after the abortive September offensive of 1915, he remarked: "I doubt whether it will ever be possible to make a serious offensive on the Western Front: too many trenches, too much barbed wire, concrete, artillery, on one side and the other. What is called the 'break-through,' what the public sees in this word — I don't believe in it. As for the war of attrition, are we making it against the Germans or they against us?"

His prescience was equally striking in other directions. When the Goeben and the Breslau sailed through the Dardanelles, he declared: "We ought to follow immediately on their heels. If not, Turkey will be in arms against us." As early as February 1915 he proposed the expedition to Salonika — to use it, however, not for an advance into the mountainous Balkans, but as a base for a march upon Constantinople with an army strong enough to encourage the Greeks and Bulgars to join with the Entente. This, one may remark, was the route which Milne took in October 1918 — a menace which hastened the surrender of Turkey. After taking Constantinople, Gallieni proposed an advance up to the Danube into Austria-Hungary in conjunction with the Rumanians. Moreover, he gave the warning that if the Allies did not go in force to Salonika the Bulgars and Greeks would turn against them. In October the Bulgars attacked Serbia.

The project of this expedition, for the command of which Gallieni was naturally designated, collapsed through the opposition of Joffre, who declared that he could not be answerable for the security of the Western Front if troops were taken away — although he found ample for the prodigal assaults in Artois and Champagne. Consulted by Briand, he even said that the idea was due to Gallieni's personal ambition to have a command. "I will not give a man. Why seek elsewhere and far away for what I shall obtain in March? I am certain to break through and drive the Germans back to their own country." But in the autumn the futility of the Western Front operations combined with the entry of Bulgaria and the sacrifice of Serbia to bring about a political crisis, forcing a reconstruction of the Government in order to inspire public confidence. Gallieni was called to be Minister of War, although protesting that he had neither the political finesse nor the health to stand the strain.

Only a few weeks before, Joffre had issued a belated citation of Gallieni's service at the Marne, a citation so diminuendo that it could only have been intended to damn by faint praise and to check the volume of public acclamation of Gallieni's services. It sought to give the impression that Gallieni had been merely a cog in the machine directed by the Commander in Chief, contributing a useful but minor share as assigned. But it was too subtle, thwarting its own purpose by the storm of indignation which its slighting phrases raised. Many urged Gallieni not to accept the citation, but he replied that indiscipline was the inherent fault of the time and the nation, and that France could only be saved if those in high places set an example in reëstablishing discipline.

A few weeks later the position was reversed and Gallieni became Joffre's superior. What a turning of the tables, what a chance for revenge! And if ever reprisal was justified it was in Gallieni's case. Yet, as four years before he had refused the succession to Michel because he had helped to unseat him, so now he refused to use his power against the man who had treated him so badly, although a large section of opinion was clamant for Joffre's dismissal and Gallieni had only to raise his finger to bring it about. Instead, his moral grandeur was attested by the way he not only strove to meet all Joffre's material needs but generously defended him in the Chamber of Deputies. Gallieni's scrupulous sense of responsibility not to abuse his power was a handicap, leading him to make extra allowance for the failings of one who had used him badly. At the same time, his loyal support was also due to the opinion that Joffre's world-wide prestige, however ill deserved, was an asset not lightly to be discarded. Knowing the tide of criticism which was rising against Joffre, Gallieni tried to reason with this stubborn and jealous despot, to induce him to make reforms which would pacify the critics and contribute to greater efficiency. As a further step Gallieni caused Joffre to be named Commander in Chief of all the French armies and appointed de Castelnau

Chief of the General Staff, sending him to headquarters, as a means of conserving Joffre's prestige
while enabling a quicker brain to influence operations.
But this remedy was marred by the passive resistance
of Joffre and his entourage, who ignored de Castelnau's presence as far as possible.

In December Colonel Driant, a Deputy, returned
on leave from the front and exposed the neglected
state of the Verdun defenses. Gallieni, who had already been disquieted by similar reports, wrote to
Joffre for an assurance that the deficiencies would be
rectified. Joffre replied in such a tone of pontifical
infallibility and rebuke that even Gallieni was nettled
and would have asserted his authority if his colleagues in the Cabinet, anxious not to precipitate a
crisis, had not persuaded him to send a soothing
answer for the moment. France paid heavily for
postponing this political crisis. Gallieni, however,
had worries enough, striving on the one hand to
protect the Higher Command from continual parliamentary and press attacks, while, on the other,
working to reform it without an upheaval, and also
occupied in trying to speed up the supply of munitions and the training of fresh troops. A sick man,
he drove himself unsparingly in order to "simplify
and accelerate" the cumbrous machinery of his own
Ministry of War, fighting the civil servants in the
battle against red tape, cutting down the mass of
"paper" which so often replaces action in the offices

of a bureaucracy, ensuring a greater interchange between the staff and the trenches, giving a human touch to the military Moloch.

The clouds on this horizon were just beginning to disperse when the storm broke at Verdun — and the vivid play of the German lightning revealed beyond concealment the unreadiness and negligence of Joffre. The country cried out, but the Cabinet could only quiver, discuss, and adjourn. Gallieni could no longer bear to watch them shivering on the brink of a decision, and resolved to push them in. Through sleepless nights, racked by pain, he had been thinking out his scheme for the reorganization of the system of command, and on March 7, 1916, he brought the memorandum to the Cabinet. It laid down that the Government ought to assume the higher control and coördination of the war in the financial, economic, diplomatic, and military aspects; that the war must be recognized as a gigantic siege and treated accordingly; that the administration of the military resources should be restored to the Ministry of War, leaving the command of the field armies free to concentrate on the conduct of operations in conformity with, but not as hitherto in disregard of, the war policy laid down by the Government. The memorandum dealt with principles and not with persons, but to fulfill these principles Gallieni proposed to bring Joffre, as Commander in Chief of all the French armies, back to

Paris, and to place de Castelnau in executive command of the field army on the Western Front. The Cabinet, although many had been vociferous in their complaints about Joffre, were panic-stricken when asked to translate their opinions into action. Finding that they would not take his advice, Gallieni resigned, showing them a medical certificate, hitherto disregarded, that it was essential that he should have two months' complete rest. Instantly they were full of protests, declaring it was impossible: "Think of Verdun! We are in the midst of battle." Gallieni scathingly replied: "Pardon, we have been at war for eighteen months, and all that time 'at war' has been battle. Moreover, it was in the midst of battle that the executive command at Verdun was changed. It was also in the midst of battle that in August 1914 the military government and defense of Paris were entrusted to me. One can take, one has always taken such measures in the midst of battle."

His colleagues' arguments beat in vain against his inflexible determination. They suggested that he should take his rest, merely dealing with vital papers, and return when fit. He told them that he was undergoing an operation which, if successful, would restore his full activity and make him fit for active service; then the Government could make use of him as it wished — but he would never return to the Ministry of War. They begged him to take two days for reconsideration; he told them that they could have an interval of grace to find a convenient explanation to tell the public. Ten days later his resignation was officially announced on the ground of ill health. Eight months later, after a summer and autumn during which hundreds of thousands of lives had been fruitlessly sacrificed, the Government carried out the reform of the Higher Command for which he had pleaded. But Gallieni was gone. Although the doctors had declared that he needed four or five months' rest to become fit for the operation, he could not bear to remain idle while France was at war, could not bear to delay his return to her service. "Head high" — his favorite phrase — as always, he entered the hospital to be operated upon, faced the pain of successive operations without a murmur, aided the doctors by his will power in the battle for his life, and with calm fortitude announced his passing.

Many eulogies have been pronounced over his grave; in 1921 he was created Marshal of France posthumously in recognition of the fact that "without Gallieni victory would have been impossible"; but the finest epitaph, and that most acceptable surely to him, is also the simplest: "Gallieni — la tête haute."

HAIG OF BEMERSYDE

THE ESSENCE OF BRITAIN

HAIG OF BEMERSYDE

THE ESSENCE OF BRITAIN

WHEN Britain for the first time in her history waged war not with a small professional army but with the nation in arms, it was characteristic of her nature that, instead of a genius, the man called to lead her armies should be the embodiment of her normal virtues and defects. Military genius has occasionally flowered on her soil, but it has been an exotic growth. Haig, in contrast, was distilled essence of Britain. Calm unimaginative acceptance of whatever fate may have in store, serene faith that all will come right in the end, resisting power deep-rooted in the tradition of centuries — these combine to produce that inexhaustible endurance which has ever been the despair of foes, sapping their own will to conquer. Marvelously apt, both for Haig and for the men of whom he was the leader and type, was the family motto of the Haigs, "Tyde what may."

Born on June 19, 1861, at Cameronbridge, Fifeshire, Douglas Haig sprang from a branch of the famous border Haigs of Bemersyde.

He conformed to the national tradition from the first. In his school and university days, at Clifton and at Oxford, he was known for his athletic powers and character, but not for any academic promise or achievements. From Oxford he went to the Royal Military College, Sandhurst, — not direct to a commission like the present-day university entrant, — and here revealed the first signs of distinction. Industry is the proverbial birthright of the Lowland Scot, and heredity may have asserted itself to give his mind a serious bent, coupled with the fact that he entered later and thus was several years older than his fellows. It is at least certain that one of his officers, in answer to an inquiry, said: "There is a cadet here called Douglas Haig, who is top at everything — books, drill, riding, sports, and games; he is to go into the Cavalry; and what is more, he will be top of the Army before he has finished." He actually passed first out of Sandhurst and was commissioned in the 7th Hussars. The Cavalry, in those days particularly, did not take soldiering too seriously, and an officer with a zest for work could be sure of receiving the grateful surrender of others' modest portion so long as he did not disturb their tranquillity. Thus after barely three years' service he became adjutant of his regiment, and this position, backed by his strong character, enabled him to disturb others to such good effect that the training of the 7th Hussars began to set new standards in India. He was helped by his skill at polo, for the fact that on joining he went straight into the 7th Hussars team, then the finest in the army, dissipated the prejudice which attaches to that unpopular species, the bookworm.

Polo, greatest of all games, is undoubtedly good training for a cavalry troop or squadron leader. But in the British army it is more, for anyone who attends regimental dinners knows that a good polo player is *ipso facto* a good general. The reason apparently does not lie, however, in the rapidity and skill of manœuvre which it induces, for I recall an interchange of such sentiments, and compliments between two distinguished cavalry generals, one of whom then went on to deliver the interesting if unhistorical dictum that "a great army can only be worn down by hard fighting; it cannot be outmanœuvred." As, under Haig, he was primarily responsible for the offensive at Ypres in 1917, hard enough in cost and result, he ought to know.

Haig's strenuous time as adjutant merely gave him a greater thirst for military experience, and he spent his subsequent leave in visits to the German army and the French Cavalry School at Saumur, his report on which brought him to wider notice. But for a moment his career was in jeopardy through the discovery that he was color-blind. Rejected in the medical examination for the Staff College, he managed to enlist the sympathy and influence of the Duke of Cambridge, who secured his entry as an exception to the rule. Haig was fortunate, for if "hard cases make bad law," an uncompromising insistence on red-tape regulations has lost the army many good soldiers.

At the Staff College, prophecy from many quarters forecast for him a great career, and fortune befriended him by providing in the quick succession of the Sudan and South African campaigns not merely a chance to win his spurs, but an extended opportunity for distinction. Coming back from the Sudan in 1899, to become brigade major to the Cavalry Brigade under Sir John French, he naturally found a place on his staff when the South African War broke out a few months later. Soon he became Chief Staff Officer to French in the Cavalry Division, where his methodical instincts, caution, and sagacity acted as ballast to his impetuous commander. Brevet promotions came rapidly, and in the later phase of the war he became commander of a group of columns during the "sweeping" operations. Here he did useful work, but the thoroughness and method which made him an ideal staff officer were not all-sufficient qualities in the chase of slippery bands of Boer partisans.

Among many honors which the campaign had brought him was that of Extra Aide-de-Camp to the King. Although his spells of home service had been short, he had won the personal regard of King Edward, and the royal interest in his career was strengthened by his marriage in 1905 to the Honorable Dorothy Vivian, one of Queen Alexandra's maids of honor. When this took place he was once more holding an appointment abroad, for in the autumn of 1903 he was appointed Inspector General of Cavalry in India, at the direct request of Kitchener, then Commander in Chief, on whom his work in the Sudan campaign had made a lasting impression. The appointment was exceptional for one who was only a brevet colonel, and coupled with his substantive promotion he was made temporary major general. Next year this rank was made permanent — an amazing rise for a man of forty-two who had only entered the army at twenty-three. He was commonly called "Lucky" Haig and, marked as was his ability, he was the favorite of fortune not merely in his escapes from death but in the combination of circumstances which gave him such a close series of opportunities to win distinction and attract notice. That he nearly climbed to a still loftier place has been revealed by Lord Esher, who presided over the committee which recast the organization of the army and created the General Staff in 1905. "The personality of General Haig, then only forty-four years old and very junior in the army, had so impressed itself upon the British Government that there was a wish to appoint him as Chief of the General Staff, making the appointment practically permanent, as was the custom in the German army. But the prejudices of seniority and rank were too great, and an older officer was named."

In India, Haig's régime was like an east wind, bracing but severe. He set a hard standard both in training and in conditions, conducting staff rides and exercises under conditions as near as possible to the reality of war — as he conceived it. That he developed the efficiency of the cavalry is unquestionable. But, like Foch, he did not fit his theories to modern facts. Despite the experience of the South African and Russo-Japanese wars, he declared himself the champion of the *arme blanche* and of shock tactics, and was so determined and sure of his opinion that he did not hesitate to remove subordinates who dared to maintain more realistic views. Basing himself on history, he was convinced, rightly, that the cavalry charge had ever been the decisive instrument of the Great Captains. His failure was that he could not, or would not, realize that modern firearms had made the cavalry charge impossible in its traditional form, and that this essential factor could only be revived by finding a substitute for the excessively vulnerable horse.

In 1906 he came home to be successively Director of Military Training and Director of Staff Duties at the War Office. Three years later he went out to India again, as Chief of the Staff, although very reluctant to take the post because of his conviction that a war with Germany was inevitable and imminent, and his wish to be on hand to take part. It was a relief to him when in 1912 he was again brought back, this time to receive the blue ribbon of home commands — the Aldershot Command. Aldershot was the main training ground of the Expeditionary Force, containing its first two divisions, and fate gave him only two years in which to prepare this force for its great test.

In 1912, as commander of an army corps, he opposed General Grierson in the army manœuvres around Cambridge, which through ill-planned direction suffered in realism. For this reason comparisons were not altogether fair, but in the military world Haig's reputation suffered a little from being outmanœuvred. The official report on his part in the manœuvres revealed in him that same obstinacy in adhering to fixed plans without regard to the facts, which was so marked a feature of his command in war. The result tended to increase the suspicion, raised in South Africa, that Haig was a better staff officer than commander, lacking strategic intuition and the instinct of surprise.

During the summer of 1914 Haig was absorbed in the intensive training of the troops at Aldershot and was in bivouac with them south of Aldershot at the moment when Austria's ultimatum to Serbia was delivered. On the declaration of war Haig took up his assigned position as Commander of one of the two army corps of the British Expeditionary Force. Grierson had the other, but, dying suddenly in the train, his command was given to Smith-Dorrien,

Haig's predecessor at Aldershot. In the opening
clash at Mons and the subsequent retreat, Haig, on
the right wing, bore a less severe strain than the
2nd Army Corps on the left wing, where the brunt of
the German onslaught fell. And history has shown
that the strain on Smith-Dorrien's corps was partly
owing to the action — or inaction — of Haig's corps.
The major responsibility, however, rested with General Headquarters, which failed to keep control of
the operations and to coördinate the movements
of the two army corps. This failure in turn had
its main source in the collapse of Sir John French's
Chief of Staff, General Murray, who fainted in an
inn at St. Quentin on August 26, the day of the critical battle at Le Cateau. Worse still, he recovered
sufficiently to think that he was functioning, when
actually he was still unfit. Thus during critical
days there was no firm hand on the helm.

The danger — as well as the subsequent difficulties
— was immensely aggravated by the fact that, at
the outset, the British retreat was split into two por-
tions by the forest of Mormal. This large and dense
obstacle was so close to the starting point of the
retreat that there was hardly time or space to withdraw the whole force by one flank, and Sir John
French decided, on receiving an inaccurate cavalry
report that there were no roads through the forest, to
divide his force, leaving Haig to retire by the east side
of the forest while Smith-Dorrien retired by the west.

The divergence was almost fatal, for, separating on August 24, it was not until September 1 that the two army corps joined up once more, — there was at times a gap of fifteen miles between their inner flanks, — and during that interval the 2nd Army Corps (Smith-Dorrien) came desperately close to disaster at Le Cateau. Isolated and unaided, except for the welcome reënforcements of a fresh division, Smith-Dorrien was compelled by the closeness of the enemy and the fatigue of his own troops to stand and fight at Le Cateau on August 26, disregarding the orders for a continuance of the retreat. After the check to the German advance caused by this rearguard action, the further retirement of the Expeditionary Force was never seriously threatened. But it was fortunate for the British troops, exhausted and disordered, that the Germans were slow to begin the pursuit and then took the wrong direction in the belief that the British were retreating westward instead of southward. This German delusion, held even before Le Cateau, was strengthened by the very fact that they only met resistance on the left wing, as Haig's corps had continued its retreat while Smith-Dorrien was standing to fight. In consequence the Germans not only attacked Smith-Dorrien's front from the north, believing that it was his flank, but passed round his right and attacked his exposed flank, believing that it was his front.

Why had Haig laid bare his neighbor's flank and

why was he too far away to support him when attacked? It has long been one of the mysteries of the war. The cause lay partly in French's failure to keep touch with and control over his two corps, partly in Haig's breach of French's original orders. On the eve of Le Cateau French had ordered both corps to continue the retreat next day in a *south-westward* direction. Smith-Dorrien, as we have seen, disobeyed these orders by stopping to fight, compelled to take the decision on his own initiative because of the difficulty of communicating with French in time. Haig apparently disobeyed these orders by retiring *southward* next day, instead of southwestward, a course which took him hour by hour farther from Smith-Dorrien. But his decision may have been inspired by verbal instructions from French, who, believing that the 2nd Corps was doomed, was intent on saving what he could of the remainder of his force — himself driving to see Haig and sending messengers to the cavalry and horse artillery. The root cause of the trouble was that in the critical hours, the commander in chief was too far away for consultation or control. French had moved his headquarters back to St. Quentin, twenty-two miles distant even from Smith-Dorrien at Bertry, and with no direct telephone communication except through the railway station there.

Liaison was, indeed, the weak joint of the command, not merely inside the British force but between it and the French. At the first meeting between Sir John French and General Lanrezac, commanding the Fifth French Army on his eastern flank, a mutual antipathy had sprung up, accentuated by the barrier of language, and thereafter each took his own course without consideration of the other. If Lanrezac gave the first cause for complaint, French, after Le Cateau, thought for a moment of cutting adrift from his allies altogether, to fall back and fortify "Torres Vedras" lines near the coast — a project from which he was only dissuaded by Henry Wilson's timely use of his inimitable powers of humor and cajolery.

This lack of liaison between the Allies throughout the retreat would have been worse but for Haig's influence. As his corps was the material link between the two armies, so he himself was the personal link, and so quickly did the French liaison officers realize this that all made a point of calling first at his headquarters on their journeys to and fro between two greater headquarters. His direction of march, due south, on the day of Le Cateau may have been due to his desire to keep in touch with the French.

Similarly, when the French Fifth Army halted their retreat on August 28, Haig sent a message to Lanrezac that his troops were perfectly fit to attack and that he wished to coöperate with the French in a counterstroke. His willingness was overruled and reprimanded, however, by Sir John French, who, in face of the appeals of the French commanders, insisted on continuing the retreat, leaving the French to fight alone and lose the fruits of their success. Let it be said in fairness to Sir John French that, seeing only the local situation, he may have found it difficult to understand why Lanrezac had left him in the lurch at Mons.

Haig had a cooler temperament and a more balanced view, as well as a better understanding of the French mind. He maintained this spirit of helpfulness when in supreme command, and none had a better grasp of the vital importance of coöperation between the Allies. If General Headquarters was sometimes as notorious for its criticisms against the French as was Grand Quartier Général against the British, such tendencies were due not to Haig but to his subordinates.

In the Battle of the Marne, which turned the tide of the war, the British force had an important indirect influence, but its direct effect was small, owing to the fact that it had made an extra day's march to the south when its allies halted for the counter-offensive. But after the subsequent advance to the Aisne and the check there, the British Expeditionary Force assumed a leading rôle and was the decisive factor in thwarting the Germans' second bid for victory. The immortal resistance of Ypres was primarily a "soldiers'" battle, depending on the courage, endurance, and musketry skill of the regimental officers and men, and on timely counterattacks carried out by battalion or brigade commanders. The rôle of the Higher Command was perforce limited to their moral influence and to their efforts to cement the crumbling parts of the front by scraping reserves from other parts. Within these limits Haig proved himself an ideal defensive general. On him fell the whole conduct of the battle. His Chief still had the delusion that he was attacking when the troops were barely holding their ground, and later, when enlightenment came, was equally insistent on retreat, only to be dissuaded by the greater will-power, and perhaps the greater self-delusion, of Foch, who had been given the rôle of coördinating the action of the Allied forces around Ypres.

Haig's economic distribution of his slender strength, and his success in "puttying up" the strained and cracking front, owed much both to his cool calculation and to the forward location of his headquarters, close to the battle front. Invaluable also was the moral influence of the calm which his bearing diffused. And on the most critical day of the struggle he revived for a moment that personal element of leadership which so often turned the scales of battle in the past, before the days of scientific killing at long range. News had just come back that the Germans had made a breach in the front at Gheluvelt; the guns were necessarily falling back, stragglers and wounded trickling down the Menin road. Up the road, moving "at a slow trot, with part of his staff behind him as at an inspection," Haig was seen riding forward toward Hooge, and the sight did much to restore confidence.

When the German tide of attack at last ebbed, and the sorely depleted British ranks were refilled and expanded, the Expeditionary Force was divided into two armies, and Haig received command of the First. In this capacity he was in executive command of all the abortive attempts in 1915 to break through the trench barrier. The first was at Neuve Chapelle in March. Here a heavy concentration of artillery was secretly assembled, and an intense bombardment of half an hour's duration delivered on the German trenches, after which the artillery lengthened their range and dropped a curtain of fire to prevent the reënforcement of the enemy's battered trenches, which were rapidly overrun by the infantry. Complete surprise was obtained and most of the first positions recaptured, but control broke down, reserves were late in coming up, and the opportunity of exploiting the initial success vanished. A further factor was that the narrow frontage of attack made the breach more easy for the defenders to close; this defect was unavoidable owing to the general shortage of munitions. The cost of this experiment might have been offset by the benefit of its experience. But both Haig and the Allied Command as a whole missed the true lesson, which was the surprise obtainable by a short bombardment that compensated its brevity by its intensity. And only partially did they appreciate that the sector attacked must be sufficiently wide to prevent the defender's artillery commanding, or his reserves closing, the breach. Instead, they drew the superficial deduction that mere volume of shell fire was the key to success. Not until late in the war did they revert to the Neuve Chapelle method, and meanwhile it was left to the Germans to turn it to profit at the expense of the Russians, in the Tarnow-Gorlice break-through in May 1915.

The British offensive at Loos, in September, was a more costly failure and without any experimental value. One fault was that it was too far away from the joint French offensive in Champagne for either to react on the other, but a worse was that the British Command tried to reconcile two irreconcilable factors: they aimed at a break-through, but preceded it with a prolonged bombardment which gave away all chance of surprise. But as the initial and fundamental mistake was appreciated only by a few, the brunt of the criticism fell on Sir John French, who had held the reserves too far back and handed them over to Haig too late for the brief opening success to be exploited.

The orders of both French and Haig for Neuve Chapelle had breathed a spirit of supreme optimism,

Haig's beginning with the grandiloquent words:
"The Expeditionary Force will resume the offensive
on March 10," which seemed an inflated description
of an attack made by two divisions on a front of less
than two miles! It is still more difficult to understand the similarly distorted perspective of the orders
for Loos, which indicated far distant objectives that
the British army did not reach until the eve of the
Armistice in 1918.

While making all allowances for the new problems
created by trench-warfare conditions, — which, however, had been foreshadowed by the Russo-Japanese
War and prophesied by Monsieur Bloch, a Polish
banker, twenty years earlier, — the historians of the
future will find it difficult to understand the slowness
of the Allied generals to grasp the defensive strength
of barbed wire and machine guns. They refuted the
old proverb, "Once bitten, twice shy," for bite after
bite failed to make them shy of prognosticating success, far less of their offensive efforts. More curious
still, in a generation of soldiers nurtured on military
history, was their utter disregard of military history.
On the one hand, they disdained the principles of
surprise and concentration, which have ever been
the master keys of the Great Captains, announcing
their intentions to the enemy by days of prolonged
bombardment and attacking with a tiny fraction of
their force while the rest remained inactive. On
the other hand, while violating the principles of nor-

mal warfare, they refused to treat their operations as siege warfare. The Messines attack in 1917 was the first and almost the only British operation which was framed on a true siege-warfare basis.

The aftermath of Loos saw Sir John French relieved of his command of the British Expeditionary Force and replaced by Sir Douglas Haig. The record of his career and every outward qualification except personal magnetism marked him out for this selection. If the miscarried offensives of 1915 had brought him no credit, they had not been signalized by the appearance of any possible rival. Haig's first task was to forge the molten ore of the New Armies, which was flowing out to France, into an offensive weapon, and to sharpen its edge by trench experience and training behind the line. To gain the time required all his strength of character, and the strain became greater when the Germans attacked Verdun and in that long-drawn-out attrition offensive gradually bled the fighting strength of France. To release French reserves, Haig relieved the French army which was holding the sector around Arras, sandwiched between the British First and Third Armies. But he refused to be hurried into a relief offensive before his forces and resources were ready. Even before Verdun was assailed, he had objected to Joffre's plan for partial offensives in April and May as preparatory steps to a general Allied offensive, simultaneously with the Russians, in midsummer. It was a pity that Haig's clear sight and sound attitude in resisting the many-sided pressure and clamor for a premature stroke in aid of the French was not maintained in the conduct of his own offensive. The original plan had been for the French to attack with forty divisions on a twenty-five mile front south of the Somme, and the British to attack, with twenty-five divisions if possible, on a fourteen-mile front north of the Somme. But, as the French were drained of their strength at Verdun, so did their share in the Somme plan evaporate. Ultimately their front of attack shrank to eight miles and their force to sixteen divisions, of which only five took part at the outset. Thus the main burden was shifted to the British and remained on their shoulders for the rest of the war.

Yet Haig's aims do not seem to have been reduced in proportion to the shrinkage of his resources. True, his orders no longer ordained the unlimited objectives of Loos nor foresaw quite so rapid a break-through as had then proved a mirage. But the ultimate objectives were as far-reaching. What possible ground was there for such ambitious dreams? The plan, while disdaining the old master keys of concentration and surprise, made no pretense to provide any new key. The Fourth Army, which was to make the attack, had only seventeen divisions, with three more in reserve under Haig. The artillery concentration, of 1500 guns, was barely the equal of that of the Germans in May 1915 for their Tarnow-

Gorlice break-through, and the defenses on the Russian front a year earlier could not be compared with the German network of wire and trenches on the Somme. The Fourth Army Command made a vain protest that with the artillery available the scheme was too ambitious.

Worse still, the British had not only to attack up-hill against an enemy holding the high ground, but they had strengthened their own obstacle by their shortsighted policy of harassing the enemy continuously as a normal trench routine. For when the Germans held the dominating positions as well as a superiority in equipment and ammunition, these "worrying" tactics wore down the British troops more than the enemy — attrition on the wrong side of the balance sheet. Further, they stirred the Germans to strengthen their trench defenses, so that the British offensive came against an almost impregnable fortress instead of the relatively weak defense system which had faced the French when they held this part of the front. For the French policy, except when engaged in active operations, was "live and let live," and when their "war-weariness" troubles of 1917 are recalled, it is the highest tribute to the endurance of British troops that they endured the policy of their leaders so long.

Finally, any chance of surprise was given away, not only by the neglect to conceal the vast preparations, but by a seven-days-long bombardment.

July 1, 1916, dawned with a promise of broiling heat, and at 7 A.M. the bombardment rose to its height. Half an hour later the infantry rose from their trenches, and thousands fell, strewing No Man's Land with their bodies before the German front trench was even reached. For their opponents were the Germans of 1916, most stubborn and skillful fighters, quick to exploit their defensive assets. While the British shells flattened their trenches, they sheltered in dugouts or shell holes, and then, as the barrage lifted, dragged out their machine guns to pour an unslacking hail of bullets into the dense and rigid waves of the attackers. The Somme marked the nadir of infantry tactics, the revival of formations that were akin to those of the eighteenth century in their formalism and lack of manœuvring power. Only as the upstanding waves were broken up by the fire, and human nature, reasserting itself, formed little groups which worked forward by rushes from shell hole to shell hole, did advance become possible. The British losses on this terrible day were 60,000, the worst day's loss in the whole history of the British army, although only fourteen divisions were engaged. The only credit was earned by the skill and fortitude of the German defenders and the unquenchable courage of the New Armies of Britain. All along the attacking line these quondam civilians bore a percentage of losses such as no professional army of past wars had ever been deemed capable of suffering without being broken as an effective instrument. Yet they carried on in an equally bitter struggle for another five months.

For, on the morrow, Haig decided to pursue the attack, although at first only in the southern sector, where his troops had gained and maintained a small foothold; the French, on their flank, with slighter opposition and more flexible tactics, had penetrated rather deeper. But he fell back on a pure attrition method of petty advances so small in scale that they could only have a tardy effect, and that chiefly on the British casualty roll. If Haig had been over-ambitious and unduly optimistic before July 1, he now tended to the other extreme.

It is a moot point whether an opportunity was missed on July 1 of exploiting the partial success in the south. The Germans were badly shaken here, and if British reserve divisions were few, theirs were fewer, as their delay in counterattacking showed. But there is no doubt as to the opportunity offered, only to be lost, on July 14. In contrast to Haig, the Fourth Army Command realized that, if the attack was to be continued, bold and rapid measures were the only chance of forestalling the German reënforcements and labor which were rebuilding, in the rear, their fortified front faster than the British could break it down.

The German second line, for the moment their last serious barrier, ran a little in front of the crest of the

watershed between the Somme and the Ancre. To
wait until the British troops had carried their line
close enough for a trench assault and their flanks
were secure, as Haig wished, would have given the
Germans time to confront them with a barrier almost
as firm as the original of July 1. The Fourth Army
Command, reviving the forgotten principle of surprise, proposed a plan which, for all its risks, — calculated risks, — was more truly secure and economical of force. It was to cross the intervening
ground under cover of darkness and assault just
before daylight after a hurricane bombardment of
only a few minutes' duration. In 1916 the ideas of
a night advance and such a brief bombardment were
alike so fresh, almost revolutionary, as to be a shock
and appear to be a gamble to orthodox opinion. To
attempt the manœuvre with New Army troops, men
who had been civilians less than two years before,
made the plan seem yet more rash to those who forgot that calculated audacity is the secret of surprise,
and hence of victory. Haig was strongly opposed
to it, preferring a more limited alternative, but Rawlinson persevered, backed by the opinion of his Chief
of Staff and the confidence of the actual troop-
leaders. Unhappily, although he gained his way,
the reluctance of the Commander in Chief caused
the postponement of the attack to July 14, a delay
that was to have grave consequences. For the stroke
succeeded, slender as its weight, and that afternoon

opportunity — and open country — stretched out its arms. The gaining of High Wood, the summit of the ridge, and a break-through were within reach. But the leading troops were weary, and the only reserves were the inevitable cavalry, easily checked by an odd machine gun or two. Worst of all, the postponement had enabled the enemy to bring up fresh reserves, and as the German strength steadily swelled their hold tightened, the British hold relaxed.

Two months of costly "nibbling" followed before the crest of the ridge, so near and yet so far, was gained. By that time a fresh network of trenches had been woven in the rear, and with the early onset of the autumn rains vanished the last dim hope of a break-through. The British losses in this inverted attrition campaign had been double the German, and the only tangible result was that, with the capture of the ridge, the British had obtained the commanding observation by which their enemy had so long profited. But, once more overruling the opinion of the executive Army Command, the Commander in Chief threw away this advantage by spending the next month in fighting his way down into the valley beyond, and so doomed the troops to the misery of a winter in flooded trenches. If the German resistance was also strained, it did not prevent them from withdrawing troops to crush Rumania.

To the tragedy of lost lives and lost chances was added that of lost potentialities. For on September

15 the premature use of a handful of tanks gave away the jealously guarded secret of this newly forged key to the French deadlock, sacrificing its birthright of decisive strategic surprise for the mess of pottage of a local success. The metaphor has a satirical aptness, for military ignorance has never made a worse mess of any new weapon. The progenitors of the tank had long before sounded the warning — in a memorandum — that the secret must be preserved until masses of machines could be launched in a great surprise stroke, and that on no account should they be used in driblets as manufactured. As Haig had expressed his agreement with this memorandum in the spring of 1916, the military historian is driven to the conclusion that the tanks were literally "pawned for a song" of illusory triumph over a local success. If so, the greater prize thus lost beyond recall was a heavy forfeit to pay for an attempt to redeem some fragment of the failure on the Somme. A mere fifty-nine were used in tiny detachments of two or three tanks, their drivers insufficiently trained, the infantry untaught how to coöperate with] them, the rear preparations scant and mismanaged, the very machines themselves obsolescent because this early model was designed in accordance with specifications based on the trenches of 1915. It was little wonder that the majority broke down or became ditched. Yet those that came into action proved such a life-saving factor and moral tonic as to reveal to discern-

ing eyes that here was the key which, when properly used, would unlock the trench barrier. But the folly did not end with their misuse. Haig reported so dubiously upon them, and in letters expressed so low an opinion of their value, that Sir William Robertson, the Chief of the Imperial General Staff at home, hastened to cancel the programme of construction, and was only prevented by political intervention.

The story of 1916, as of 1917, is a painful indictment of the Commander in Chief's lack of vision and obstinate disregard of advice whose truth was borne out by the result. But it cannot be burked by the conscientious historian, even though he recognized the virtue of this very obstinacy in later crises — to which it had contributed. In Haig, physiognomy was a true index of character — the forehead, though not mean, dominated and eclipsed by the chin. So thought and imagination, although active within strict limits, were dominated by an unswerving determination which when beneficial was called tenacity, and when harmful was called obstinacy. Haig at least was far more than a Joffre — his obstinacy was due to mental limits, not to pure ignorance, and he was never the catspaw of subtler brains. And although his determination was so strong, he was not so insensible to the human cost as some of his coadjutors whose personal resolution was less. In some measure his very defects sprang from virtues. His loyalty to old comrades and long-known subordinates made him slow to remove those who failed under the test of war and its new conditions. His lack of selfish ambition prevented him from cultivating that blend of geniality and fire which to some is natural and in others an artifice, but which is the magnetism of leadership. His remoteness, combined with his inability to argue, tended to discourage all but the most resolute subordinates from pressing contrary opinions; and physical courage is a far more common virtue than moral courage among soldiers long apprenticed to the profession of arms. The Army Commanders — "the Barons" as they were commonly termed — might be awe-inspiring war-lords in their own domain, but few of them ventured to stand up to Haig. Because of his manner, more than his character, the very subordination which military discipline induces tended to become its own poison.

But public and political criticism had been growing in volume, and at the close of the Somme campaign Haig was lucky to escape the fate of his French colleagues, Joffre and Foch. Nevertheless the fall in his credit had perhaps worse consequences. For the British Government, now led by Mr. Lloyd George, lacked the courage to depose him or the confidence to support him, and so lent themselves to the baneful compromise of subordinating him to the control, in operations, of the new commander in chief of the French army — Nivelle. This violated an axiom of war and of common sense, for a general cannot

effectively direct another army while he is engrossed
in the executive command of his own. Moreover,
the atmosphere of distrust was a fertile breeding-
ground for intrigue. Early in 1917 the French produced at the Calais conference a scheme for an
amalgamated command, with a French commander
in chief, a British chief of staff, and a mixed headquarters staff. When this was rejected through
British military opposition and the other compromise
— of subordination — adopted, Nivelle's personal
staff began to intrigue in London for Haig's removal.
The chief wire-puller was Colonel D'Alenson, who,
in the confidential post of *chef de cabinet*, stood ever
at his master's elbow and wielded an irregular power
far greater than that of the official heads of the French
staff. Consumed with ambition and disease, con-
scious that his career was a race between glory and
death, this restless and able schemer urged Nivelle
on to an early and supreme gamble to win the war at
a stroke. All the more anxious was he to remove any
impediments to the fulfillment of his design and,
regarding Haig in this category, he sought to supplement his underground attack by a series of dicta-
torial instructions, their tone hardly civil, to Haig,
in the hope that resentment might produce a crisis
and Haig's resignation. In this object D'Alenson
failed, and even the temporary harm he did to Allied
relations was minimized by Haig's own balance of
mind, for if stung to complain he was not stung to

retaliate, and it is one of the highest tributes to him that although sorely tried he never let his sense of injury obscure his sense of the need for coöperation between the Allies. It is a question whether a fine sense of duty should have prompted Haig to resign when he felt that he no longer possessed the confidence of his Government or his Allies, and that his troops might suffer in consequence — as they did in April 1917 and March 1918. But it is beyond question that no man has shown or maintained greater self-control in face of the storms of criticism and the undercurrents of intrigue.

Nivelle's appointment caused a change and, worse still, a delay in the original plan of campaign for 1917. Before it could begin the Germans had disrupted its foundations by a strategic withdrawal from the huge Somme salient which the Allies had planned to pinch out. Straightening their front by retiring to the newly fortified Hindenburg Line, the Germans left their foes to follow laboriously through the intervening desert which, with immense thoroughness of destruction, they had created. By nullifying the Allies' preparations for attack, this withdrawal dislocated the initial moves in their plan, and restricted them to the sectors on the two flanks of the evacuated area. Thus they had to launch their main blows before the enemy's reserves were pinned down by pressure elsewhere.

The British struck first, in the north near Arras,

on April 9. The temporary check to the supply of tanks had left a hurricane bombardment as the only means of achieving a surprise, but although Allenby, commanding the Third Army, urged such a course, the timely removal — by promotion — of his artillery adviser cleared the way for the long-drawn-out method which the Higher Command preferred. Three weeks of systematic wire-cutting followed by a five-days bombardment gave the Germans ample warning and the usual results followed. After sweeping over the forward positions which their shells had razed, the attackers were brought to a stop by intact defenses in the rear. South of the evacuated area, the French blow in Champagne, on April 16, was equally abortive in strategic results and, because of its greater scale, a greater fiasco. The excessive hopes raised by Nivelle caused the greater reaction, and to the accompaniment of mutinies among the slaughter-weary French troops, Nivelle fell from power, to be replaced by Pétain and a more cautious policy, and for the rest of the year the British bore almost the entire burden of the campaign.

With the failure of the French any chance of a beneficial reaction on the dying British offensive at Arras vanished. But Haig decided to continue the operations in order, as he explained at a conference of army commanders on April 30, to reach a "good defensive line." If these later attacks were modest in scale of force and objective, they were extravagant in lives. Haig's advocates have thrown the blame partly on the faulty tactics of the Third Army Command in face of the new defensive tactics of the Germans — thinly held forward positions with reserves concentrated in rear for prompt counterattack — and partly on the unfulfilled promises of the French to continue their pressure. If there is much truth in these contentions, it is not the whole truth. For the minutes of the Conference on April 30 reveal, first, that Haig placed little reliance on the prospect of the French continuing their attacks, and, secondly, that the prolongation of the Arras offensive was based on a local object and not dictated by that of bringing relief to the French.

After the costly failure, early in May, to reach this "good defensive line," Haig decided to transfer the main weight of his attack into Belgium, as he had originally intended to do at an earlier date. His loyalty to his allies, and his sense of the common interest, inspired him to press on with this offensive policy even though French coöperation was lacking. And it is just to recognize that at this juncture the British Prime Minister, who had committed himself to the Nivelle gamble, was equally ardent to pursue the offensive, although on cooler reflection he subsequently tried, in vain, to check the policy which he had countenanced.

But if the ominous situation of the French army, the crisis at sea caused by the submarine campaign, and the need to second the still possible Russian offensive, combined to justify Haig's decision in May, the situation had changed well before the attack was launched at the end of July. In war all turns on the time factor. By July the French army was recuperating, if still convalescent, the height of the submarine crisis was past, and the revolutionary paralysis of the Russian army was clear. Nevertheless, Haig would not change his plans.

And as a preparatory step, the Messines ridge south of Ypres had been secured by the Second Army, under Plumer, with Harington as chief of staff. For once, in a siege war, the attack was carried out according to engineer experience. The explosion of long-prepared mines, the discharge of a great volume of gas, the dovetailed coöperation between artillery, tanks, and infantry, were features of a meticulously organized scheme which by its economical success proved a model example of the true siege-warfare attack. It was above all due to perfect staff-work, and thus corresponded with the conditions of what was essentially a "staff officers' and engineers' war," in all armies.

But in the greater operation which followed, not only the principle but the method and the choice of site were open to criticism. The axis of the attack diverged from, instead of converging on, the German main communications, so that the advance could not vitally endanger the security of the enemy's position in France. Haig was to adopt here the same *eccentric* direction of advance which a year later his advice prevented Foch and Pershing from taking. And if the advance on the Belgian coast could yield no wide strategic results, the idea that it was necessary in order to capture the German submarine bases on this coast has long since been exploded, for the main submarine campaign was conducted from German ports. It is just, however, to emphasize that this mistaken belief was impressed on Haig by the Admiralty.

But, worst of all, the Ypres attack was doomed before it began, by its own destruction of the intricate drainage system in this part of Flanders. The British Command had persevered for over two years with the method of a prolonged preparatory bombardment, believing that quantity of shells was the key to success, and that, unlike all the Great Captains of history, they could disregard the principle of surprise. The offensive at Ypres, which was finally submerged in the swamps of Passchendaele, in October, threw into stronger relief than ever before the fact that such a bombardment blocked the advance for which it was intended to pave the way, because it made the ground impassable.

The legend has been fostered that these swamps were a piece of ill luck due to the heavy rain, a natural and therefore an unavoidable hindrance that could not be foreseen. In reality, before the battle

began a memorandum was sent to General Headquarters pointing out that if the Ypres area was
destroyed by bombardment the battlefield would
become a swamp. In the disregard of this warning
is epitomized the cause of that disastrous failure,
inevitable from the outset, for the mud was hampering operations in the very first days. But in
another quarter the lesson was assimilated in three
days, instead of the three months which General
Headquarters took before they abandoned the hopeless struggle. On August 3 an alternative project
was drawn up at Tank Corps headquarters. Its preface contained this significant example of prevision:
"From a tank point of view, the Third Battle of
Ypres may be considered dead. To go on using
tanks in the present conditions will not only lead to
good machines and better personnel being thrown
away, but also to a loss of morale in the infantry
and tank crews through constant failure. From an
infantry point of view, the Third Battle of Ypres
may be considered comatose. It can only be continued at colossal loss and little gain. . . ."

The alternative proposal was for a large-scale raid
near Cambrai, where the rolling downland lent itself
to tank movement, as a dramatic means of restoring
British prestige and an economic means of keeping
the Germans occupied. The basic idea was the
release of a swarm of tanks without any preparatory
bombardment to give warning of the blow. The

proposed sector was in the area of the Third Army, now under Byng, who showed himself instantly receptive to the idea, although inclined to expand it from a raid into a definite attack. On August 6 he went to General Headquarters, saw Haig, and suggested an attack with tanks at Cambrai on September 20. The Commander in Chief was favorable, but his Chief of Staff, Kiggell, made strong objection on the ground that the army could not win a decisive battle in two places at once, and should rather concentrate every possible man in the Ypres area. Thus the enlarged idea postponed the raid, as the refusal to recognize the "writing on the wall" at Ypres postponed the attack at Cambrai until it was too late to gain decisive results.

This damping reception failed to extinguish the scheme, and late in October the growing hopelessness of the Ypres offensive rekindled the smouldering embers; ultimately, the Cambrai operation was fixed for November 20. But it had been transformed into a far-reaching offensive, aimed to penetrate as far as Valenciennes, for which the British had not the resources because of the drain at Ypres. It is extremely difficult to understand what was in mind as to the future, for, without reserves, success could only mean the creation of an excessively deep and narrow salient, requiring many divisions to hold it.

Led by nearly 400 tanks but followed by only six infantry divisions, the attack came as a complete

surprise, and despite minor checks achieved a penetration far deeper and at less cost than any previous
British offensive. But all the available troops and
tanks were thrown into the first blow, and the Higher
Command failed to give Byng the few reserves they
possessed in time to exploit the success. And the
cavalry, as always on the Western Front, belied Haig's
unfailing faith, proving unable to carry out this rôle.
Once more the British Command had failed to fit
their end to their means.

The best comment on this lack of reserves was
supplied by the commander of the neighboring French
Army Group, Franchet d'Espérey. A long motor
ride in search of information brought him to a British
headquarters at Albert. Entering, he interrogated
a senior General Staff officer, flinging at him a string
of questions as to the progress of the attack, its
frontage, depth. Then came the final, the vital
question: "And where were your reserves?" "Mon
général, we had none." The French commander
exclaimed, "Mon Dieu!" turned on his heel, and
fled. If the excuse be that the Ypres battles had
drained us of reserves, — even so, there were divisions which came up, too late, — then it surely
reflects on the choice of that swamp-like area and
the failure to try earlier the method that at Cambrai
unlocked the doors to decisive success.

For want of nourishment the advance died away,
and on November 30 a German counterstroke nearly

turned limited success into unlimited disaster. The sole fruit of Cambrai was the lesson — applied the next year.

But since early in November the stream of German troop-trains westward from the Russian front had been steadily swelling, and the British Command suddenly awoke from their offensive dreams to the grim reality that, with Russia out of the war, they and their French allies had to face almost the whole armed strength of Germany. The Italian disaster at Caporetto added to their depression and their mood veered round to one of sheer defense. But their own extravagant offensive had dissipated their resources and sacrificed their credit. If English action had relieved the strain on French resources, what was the benefit if England had drained her own to the verge of bankruptcy? And because of the loss of credit, reënforcements were withheld by a Government sick of spendthrift strategy, and dubious of the military change of mood.

The danger was aggravated by two further developments. Owing to the insistence of Clemenceau, the new French Premier, Haig was forced to extend his line and take over more of the front from the French at the moment when his reserves were at the lowest. This meant that Gough's Fifth Army was dangerously stretched out and took over ill-prepared defenses on the very sector where Ludendorff was about to strike. Secondly, Haig's innate distrust of compromises led him to take the decisive step which nullified the effort to establish a form, if an immature one, of unified control before the threatening storm broke on the Allied front. The new Supreme War Council of the Allies had planned to create an interallied general reserve, under the control of its military executive committee, of which Foch was appointed chairman. Haig, however, brought this scheme tumbling to the ground by his reply, when called on by Foch to contribute his quota of seven divisions, that he could spare no troops. He preferred to rely on a working arrangement with Pétain, his French vis-à-vis, for mutual support. But his own almost quixotic sense of loyalty and the common interest led his judgment astray, and when the German blow fell on his own front, as he had rightly forecast, he was speedily disillusioned. Perhaps also he lacked the imagination to put himself in Pétain's shoes and to make allowance for the possibility that the French commander might have an equally fixed, if incorrect, conviction that the real attack was due on his front.

When the German attack was launched on March 21 and the Fifth Army was driven back over the old Somme battlefields, Haig found that his compact with Pétain was inadequate. French reserves were slow in arriving to his assistance, and after a comfortless interview with Pétain, Haig sent an urgent call to Lord Milner, the Secretary of State for War. Milner, however, was already on his way and the outcome

of his intervention was the emergency conference of
Allied ministers and generals at Doullens on March
26. Sinking personal pride in face of the crisis, not
only did Haig back Milner's proposal that Foch
should be appointed to coördinate the combined
action of the British and French armies, but it was
on his intervention that the scope of Foch's commission was extended to the whole of the Western
Front, instead of merely "around Amiens." No one
had a more thorough appreciation of the fact that
Amiens, the junction point between the Allied armies,
was also the joint in the Allied harness which must
be covered at all costs. To no one was its security
more due. But his instinct for method also taught
him that a compromise which gave Foch partial
responsibility was impracticable, and he voluntarily
subordinated himself in order to give Foch a com-
prehensive responsibility. This loyal coöperation
was maintained throughout the last year, and carried
so far that when in July Foch pressed for British
reserves to meet the expected German blow in Champagne, Haig complied with his demands although
still expecting attack on his own front, and although
those previously sent had been sacrificed owing to
the blunders of their French commander. And in
his loyalty Haig refused the British Government's
offer of intervention.

It is perhaps a little difficult to reconcile Haig's
emphasis on guarding the Amiens "joint" with his

initial dispositions, wherein he placed most of his reserves in the north, and left to Gough's army not only the longest and most difficult sector to defend, but the lowest proportion of troops to hold it. The reason was probably that he anticipated, rightly, that the heavier weight of the German attack would fall on Byng's Third Army near Arras, and did not anticipate that if the Germans broke through they would penetrate so deeply or so rapidly as they did. And whereas the front in the north was unpleasantly close to the vital Channel ports, there was room on Gough's front to fall back some distance. It was only when the distance reached to a forty-mile withdrawal that the danger to Amiens became serious. Moreover, later knowledge reveals that Byng's successful resistance at Arras, combined with the extent of Gough's enforced retreat south of the Somme, tended to change radically the German plans, and lured Ludendorff on to his ultimate undoing.

Throughout the crisis of the German inroads, first on the Somme and then, in April, on the Lys, Haig proved the same cool and unshakable commander as at Ypres in 1914. If, because of the greater scale of his command, his control could not be so direct as in 1914, he showed the same prudent and calculating use of his reserves to "putty up" the crumbling parts of the front, and the moral symbol of his ride down the Menin road was reproduced in his immortal order of April 11 : "Many amongst us now are tired.

To those I would say that victory will belong to the side which holds out the longest. . . . There is no other course open to us but to fight it out! Every position must be held to the last man; there must be no retirement. With our backs to the wall, and believing in the justice of our course, each one of us must fight on to the end. . . ." The only shadow on these noble sentiments is the reflection that if Haig had refrained earlier from butting frontally at an impassable wall his troops might not now have had their "backs to the wall."

In this crisis, however, he strove manfully to husband life; his timely withdrawal of his line in the Ypres salient largely nullified the German blow planned at this point, and he would have made other elastic withdrawals but for Foch's opposition. When the tide turned with the great counterstroke on the Marne in July, Haig had an opportunity to show that in attack he had profited by his repeated hard lessons of earlier years. He had let Foch have British reserves for the Marne battle against the wishes of his staff, and now he was instantly receptive to suggestions from the Fourth Army Command, whom he had overruled so frequently in 1916. A small but ably conceived surprise operation with tanks on July 4 had revealed to Rawlinson and his chief of staff, Montgomery, a significant weakening in the enemy's morale and defects in his trench system. After the idea had been broached in conversation,

Rawlinson submitted to Haig on July 17 a detailed scheme for a large-scale surprise attack on the Cambrai model. Haig at once approved it in preference to an attack on the Lys, which Foch had proposed as one of a series of local offensives to free his lateral railway communications. Foch accepted the alternative site and placed under Haig the French First Army under Debeney, to extend the front of attack on the south. Rawlinson's army was secretly doubled, and by skillful precautions the enemy were kept in the dark until on August 8 the surprise attack was launched, led by 450 tanks. Great as a material success, it was still greater as a moral, for it so convinced Ludendorff of the final tilting of the scales that he informed the Kaiser that peace ought to be sought without delay.

On August 10 — when the advance was slowing down, but a new attack, by Humbert's army, was beginning on Debeney's right — Foch issued orders to Haig for Rawlinson and Debeney to continue their attack while Byng's army was to prepare to strike in on Rawlinson's left. Haig, now imbued with the principle of economizing life, objected to an immediate continuation of Rawlinson's direct advance against stiffening resistance, but agreed to launch Byng and proposed also to throw in the right of Horne's First Army, lying next to Byng. After a tussle of wills, Foch gave way. On August 17 Mangin's army struck, south of Humbert; on August 21

Byng advanced; on August 26 Horne, and on the
same day Rawlinson, began to move forward again.
The difference of opinion — and its effects — between
Haig and Foch can be and has been exaggerated.
For although marked credit is due to Haig for modi-
fying Foch's method toward economy of life, it is
clear that the basic plan of alternate "shouldering"
advances in rapid succession, the keynote of this
new strategy, had already been created by Foch.
As a result, the whole German front, Soissons to
Arras, was in a state of flux, the Germans evacuating
under pressure the areas captured in the spring, and
falling back on the Hindenburg Line. Could they
stand fast here? That was the vital problem. And
in solving it Haig's influence was more important
than in the earlier question. Method and determination, his permanent assets, were now his valuable contributions to the Allied stock. Further, it is
beyond question, if natural, that he had a more correct appreciation of the German decline than the
Government at home. At the end of August they
sent Haig a cipher telegram expressing their anxiety
if further heavy losses were to be incurred in attacking the Hindenburg Line. It is absurd, as some
have done, to blame them, for not only had the soldiers given the statesmen just cause for anxiety in
the past, but, as armed forces are based on the
strength of the nation in rear, strategy must necessarily be the servant of policy. At the same time it

is just to recognize the moral courage which Haig showed in accepting responsibility for the attack and staking his reputation on his opinion.

Foch, who had now freed his lateral railways, was able to turn to wider aims, and produced his plan for a combined general offensive. A compound British, French, and Belgian force was to attack on the left wing in Flanders; the main British force was to break the Hindenburg Line and advance toward Maubeuge, so threatening to cut the western end of the Germans' main lateral railway and their line of retreat west of the hilly forest region of the Ardennes; the French were to advance against the German centre in Champagne; the Americans to strike toward the Briey coal fields, just west of Metz, and the eastern end of the German lateral railway. If rapidly successful, this last stroke promised decisive results in cutting the German line of retreat east of the Ardennes and turning the possible German line of resistance along the French frontier. But it diverged from the direction of the other attacks and so would not have the same reaction upon them as a converging advance. Haig, more prudent, urged Foch to alter this into a converging advance toward Mézières, and Foch agreed to the change.

Here again, although ardent partisans have exploited the modification to exalt Haig and depreciate Foch, the effect can be exaggerated. For, in the first place, the British broke through the renowned defenses of the Hindenburg Line without the Mézières attack drawing off any material fraction of the German resistance which faced them. At the outset of this battle there were 57 German divisions opposing 40 British and 2 American divisions on the Hindenburg Line. For the Mézières advance there were 31 French and 13 larger-strength American divisions — a total equivalent to at least 60 normal Ally divisions — against 20 enemy divisions.

Secondly, after breaking through the German defenses, the Allies' converging advance lost impetus owing to the difficulty of supply over the destroyed areas, and by the date of the Armistice all hope had vanished of cutting off the main German forces. And when the curtain fell on the long drama of the Western Front, Foch was about to launch, although a little farther east, the Franco-American turning manœuvre which he had originally intended for September, and which was now the only chance of retrieving the hope of a decisive military victory.

It is right to put forward these facts to restore a balanced view, but they in no way depreciate the real services which Haig rendered in his own sphere by directing the vital operations which, by breaking the Hindenburg Line, hastened the German decision to capitulate.

As in an earlier phase his virtue of loyalty had the effect of a vice, so in the last phase his vice of ob-

© *Underwood & Underwood*

HAIG CONGRATULATING CANADIAN TROOPS, SEPTEMBER 1918

stinacy became a virtue. Like Foch, he had profited by experience, and like Foch also, his profit was greatly increased because in the last phase, when the balance of numbers and morale turned definitely in his favor, the conditions at last came to fit his theories even more than his theories moved to meet the conditions.

He was different from Foch in that, while Foch stands out in relief from the background of war, vital in interest as a man apart from his association with great events, Haig is engraved in the face of the war, and because of inherent self-effacement his career must be traced through the course of events.

As an executive commander there has hardly been a finer defensive general; in contrast, among those who have earned fame as offensive generals none perhaps have made worse errors. In the last phase he did much to regild his reputation, but the scope for more than method and determination was not wide. His mind was dominated by the instinct of method, a valuable asset; where he failed was in the instinct of surprise in its widest sense — originality of conception, fertility of resource, receptivity to ideas. And without the instinct of surprise, the key to economic and decisive success in war, no man can take rank among the Great Captains. But as a great gentleman, — also in the widest sense, — and as a pattern of noble character, Haig will stand out in the roll of history, *chevalier sans peur et sans reproche*, more spotless by far than most of Britain's national heroes. Most of all, perhaps, because in his qualities and defects he was the very embodiment of the national character and the army tradition.

FERDINAND FOCH

THE SYMBOL OF THE VICTORIOUS WILL

FERDINAND FOCH

THE SYMBOL OF THE VICTORIOUS WILL

LIKE Joffre, Foch was born under the shadow of the
Pyrenees — at Tarbes on October 2, 1851. And
like Joffre also, as well as Ludendorff, his great opponent to be, he was of bourgeois family, thus truly
symbolical of the war of peoples. Symbolism,
indeed, is the texture of his whole career, so abun-
dantly woven of it that there is ample material for
legend, for future generations to behold in him one
destined by Providence to be the symbol and savior
of the Allied nations in the war. The fact of his
birthplace being Tarbes was due to the exigencies of
the civil-service career of his father — whose Christian name was Napoléon, — for the family came
from Valentine, near St. Gaudens, and were reputed
to spring from the old Celtiberian stock of Ariège.
There was even a mystical significance in the fact
that the arms of Valentine, unique in the French
provinces, are akin to those of the old kingdom of
France, fleurs-de-lis, surmounted by a crown, — forecast of victory? — supported by a lion, — emblem
of courage or of England in alliance? — and flanked
by two angels. These may perhaps be regarded as

spiritualized versions of the American eagle or as the guardian angels which at several periods preserved Foch from the danger threatened by his German foes or French detractors, as well as from the consequences of his own errors.

Despite his father's Christian name, the family had been associated more with commercial and municipal than with military affairs, but a martial tradition came down to the boy on his mother's side, for her father was an officer in the Napoleonic army who had won the Legion of Honor in the Peninsular War.

Ferdinand's school career suffered at first from his father's changes of station, but when at fifteen he went to the Jesuit college at St. Étienne, he made rapid progress and his report said: "Esprit géométrique. À l'étoffe d'un polytechnicien." This verdict decided his career. The Polytechnique, it is necessary to mention, is not merely a training school for the artillery and engineers, but the gateway to most of the higher posts in the civil service, and its examination is one of the hardest in France. Therefore, after taking his *baccalauréat*, Foch went in 1869 to the Jesuit college at Metz, which had a notable record for successes in the Polytechnique entrance examination. On the outbreak of the Franco-German War next year he enlisted in the infantry, but the Armistice came before he had seen any fighting, and he returned to the college at Metz, which was now occupied by the Germans, and thus he was present when the trium-

FOCH

phant salvos of artillery hailed the cession to Germany of the city which he was destined to restore to France.

Passing into the Polytechnique that same year, he passed out of it into the artillery before his course was complete, owing to the urgent need of officers in the reconstructed army, a shortage which helped him to rapid promotion — in 1878 he became captain in a regiment stationed at Rennes. While there he married a Mlle. Julie Bienvenue at St. Brieuc, a marriage which brought him also the possession of an old Breton château at Ploujean, where he subsequently spent most of his periods of leave. Passing into the École Supérieure de Guerre in 1885, he passed out fourth, and after alternate staff and regimental soldiering, the second turning point of his career came on October 31, 1895, when he returned to the Staff College as professor.

During the next five years he made his name as the leading military thinker among the younger school, and by his teaching exercised a vital influence not only on the future leaders of the French army but on the war drama of 1914. His lectures were enshrined in two military classics, *Des Principes de la Guerre* and *De la Conduite de la Guerre*, which have been to many military students outside France their first guide in the labyrinths of war study. Incidentally, the preface of the second was concluded with the prophetic words: "In memoriam, in spem."

The efforts of French military writers since 1870 had been devoted to searching for Napoleon's secret recipe for victory. One after another claimed its discovery. But while most of them tended to produce some geometrical formula of manœuvre, Foch, the former "esprit géométrique," found instead a psychological secret: "The will to conquer sweeps all before it. There is a psychological phenomenon in great battles which explains and determines their result. One hundred thousand men leave ten thousand of their number dead on the ground and acknowledge themselves beaten; they retreat before the victors, who have lost as many men if not more. Neither one side nor the other knows, when they fall back, what its own losses have been nor how heavy those of the opposing force, therefore, it is not on account of material damage, still less from any possible computation of figures, that the loser gives up the struggle." And the lesson drawn by Foch is contained in his favorite quotation from Joseph de Maistre: "A lost battle is a battle which one believes lost; in a material sense no battle can be lost." Hence Foch deduced: "If defeat comes from moral causes, victory may come from moral causes also, and one may say, 'A battle won is a battle we will not acknowledge to be lost.'"

Foch was surely born to command British troops of whom their foes have complained that they "refuse to know when they are beaten." But he relied more on the will of the commander than of the troops. "What compels victory is, above all else, the conduct of the commander. 'Cæsar and not the Roman legions conquered Gaul,' said Napoleon, and Rome trembled before Hannibal, not because of the Carthaginian soldiery." At the same time Foch was distinguished by a practical common sense, embodied in his constant remark, "*De quoi s'agit-il? —* What is the problem?" His lectures contrasted the strategy of Napoleon with that of Moltke, showing that the Germans in 1870 adopted a preconceived plan which lacked the flexibility necessary for its adjustment to the enemy's movements. And, added to this initial defect, they failed to make the thorough reconnaissance or dispositions to guarantee the security of this plan — to secure their own freedom of action in face of enemy interference. Luckily for the Germans, the foe of 1870 was supine and his strategy purposeless, but even so they met with surprise after surprise, from which they were extricated and carried through to victory by the superior fighting powers of the subordinate leaders and their troops.

From his comparative study of the German errors on the one hand and Napoleon's campaigns on the other, Foch acquired a conviction of the essential importance of the principle of security and of the need to "fix" the enemy by reconnaissance and fighting, as a preliminary to any manœuvre. To use the metaphor of personal combat, one must grip the

enemy by the throat before attempting the knock-
out blow — which may otherwise hit the air.　From
his teaching, too, emerges another axiom which is
important because it gives us a clue to his action in
1918.　Because of his "de quoi s'agit-il," his emphasis on facts, his disbelief in preconceptions, and his
view of war's ever changing situations, he leaned
toward opportunism in execution — making the
most of the moment in the belief that the morrow
will take care of itself.

Finally, his almost mystical belief in the will to
conquer led him to an extreme, perhaps an excessive,
emphasis on the value of the offensive.　"Never can
the defensive lead to the enemy's destruction, never
can it achieve the conquest of the ground he occu-
pies, though this may be the single exterior sign
of victory."　His studies give little heed to the
defensive-offensive: Wellington he ignores and Aus-
terlitz he neglects.

The essence of Foch's teaching was thus a powerful
reassertion of the moral factor, particularly in the
leader, combined with a masterly calculation of the
time and space factors as a means to security and
hence to his end — the decisive manœuvre.　But it
is void of any discussion of, or interest in, material
factors such as armament, or the effect of weapons
and their development upon strategy and tactics.　A
side light on the limitations of his pre-war outlook is
contained in his remark at the Circuit de l'Est in 1910,

which proved the reliability of the aëroplane. "That is good sport, but, for the army, the aëroplane is nought." Further, he was engrossed in the morale of the leader and did not pause to meditate upon the influence of superior or inferior weapons — on the morale of the led. And because of this his doctrine, for all its excellence, which he had intended as "a bonfire lighted on a dangerous coast to assist doubtful navigators," actually led the navigators of France military among rocks where they nearly foundered. For the rising generation of military thought, running to extremes as is the way of disciples, exalted the will to conquer into a catch-phrase panacea for victory, and, imbued with the offensive, came to believe that they had only to attack to conquer. Thus it was left for August 1914 to show that bullets — hard facts — can overcome will, through shattering the bodies of the soldiers if not of the general.

Lieutenant-Colonel Foch left the École de Guerre in 1900, but seven years later returned to it as commandant. He had just been promoted to general of brigade in 1907 when Clemenceau, the new premier, sent for him and offered the post. The names of Foch and Lanrezac had been submitted to Clemenceau and, in order to decide, the Prime Minister sent for the lectures of the two men, and after reading them made his choice, preferring the philosophical style of Foch to the realistic style of Lanrezac — who in August 1914 was to be "the voice crying in the wilderness" that the Germans would come through western Belgium.

Foch had quitted his professorship in 1900, owing partly to the anticlerical storm which was raging, and in view of Clemenceau's radical views he thought fit to remind the Premier that his brother was a priest. The objection was waved aside with a forcible comment that all Clemenceau cared was that Foch should be capable of reorganizing the school. The meeting was a foretaste of their future association in a greater effort, with results as happy but relationships less so.

In this congenial work Foch remained for four years. In 1911, promoted to general of division, he left to take up an active command, the 13th Division, from which only a year later he was advanced to command of the 8th Army Corps at Bourges. But the best proof that he was regarded not merely as a brilliant theorist was that in 1913 he was given charge of the famous 20th Army Corps, which formed part of the frontier-covering force, maintained at full strength during peace. On July 18, 1914, Foch went on leave to his Breton château. Recalled when the emergency came, it fell to him to taste the first bitter fruits of the misguided Plan XVII and the mad *offensive à outrance* doctrine of which his teaching had been the seed. Let it be said, however, that as he had no share in formulating the plan, so his theories of the offensive had been pressed to a reductio ad absurdum by de Grandmaison and his school, who, with the support of Joffre and de Castelnau, now swayed the military mind of France. Foch and his teachings indeed were démodé, and his emphasis on the principle of security was regarded as a want of faith in the irresistible élan of the French soldier. To this loss of influence over the rising generation his own manner contributed. Always a deep rather than a clear thinker, his philosophical treatment of war tended to become mystical as he became more senior, and he spoke in parables which often took days for his officers to fathom. Once, at a conference after an exercise, his summing up consisted simply of one vehement sentence hurled at a commander : "If you arrive at the station two or three minutes after the train has gone, you miss it." He rarely stooped to explain, and allowed no deviation from his own views. With the officers he neither sought nor attained popularity and to the men he was simply a symbol. Even if he was aware that some of his mystified subordinates declared him insane, he did not mind, for to him morale connoted his own soul, and knowing that, he was content.

The 20th Corps, as part of de Castelnau's Second Army, moved forward with the premature French advance into Lorraine and on August 19 suffered as heavily as any in the vain assault on the Morhange position. In the rapid retreat which followed, Foch's corps was markedly steady. Moreover, when the

French stood at bay along the Grand Couronne, covering Nancy and the "gap of Charmes," the 20th Corps delivered a counterstroke against the German flank which largely helped to make the Germans abandon their offensive for the moment. At this juncture Foch himself was called away to a higher rôle.

The French general offensive had failed everywhere, and the French armies had begun the great retreat which ended on the Marne. In the left centre a gap threatened to open between the Fourth Army and the Fifth, which was the flank army next to the British. To fill the gap, Joffre had decided to improvise a new Ninth Army, made up at first merely by dividing the Fourth Army, if later reënforced from Lorraine. Foch was given the command, and, in turn, had to improvise a staff, and naturally had to take officers who were not already occupied in pivotal posts. As he himself said later, "We were like a poor household. There was a staff of five or six officers hastily got together, little or no working material, only our notebooks and a few maps." But he was fortunate in his first choice, for a chief of staff. In the 20th Corps at the time, serving as second in command of a cavalry regiment, there was an officer named Maxime Weygand, who, although not a Staff College graduate, had marked himself out for early distinction. As an instructor at the Cavalry School at Saumur, the lucid reasoning and striking common sense which underlay his lectures had spread his reputation, and many of his contemporaries had come to regard him as the ablest of their generation.

When Weygand first came to Foch he was sorely tried by his chief's disconcerting ways, but gradually the two blended and ultimately became inseparable, mounting together until they established themselves as one of the immortal combinations of history. They have been compared with Napoleon and Berthier, and with Hindenburg and Ludendorff. Neither comparison is accurate. Weygand was as ideal a staff officer as Berthier, but he was much more — to an amazing memory and capacity for detail he added strength of character, initiative, and originality. But, unlike Ludendorff, he did not obscure, or superimpose himself upon, his chief. To the world, he sank himself completely in his chief, and to those who sought to probe beneath the surface replied that all the credit belonged to Foch. It is, however, at least sure that he was the essential complement of Foch, supplying the qualities his chief lacked. Weygand had the power to translate Foch's mystical phrases into practical and clear directions, and was a born organizer, whereas Foch was a natural disorganizer — indeed, he seemed to many not to understand the needs and principles of either organization or training. But if Foch understood neither details nor men in the mass, he knew what men to pick and he learned how to trust them. "Weygand c'est moi," the phrase has become part of history, and there was equal truth in his nickname for Weygand, "Ma encyclopédie." His first great test was to come, and it is curious that the Battle of the Marne should have brought him into popular fame by a feat which was mythical, but which none the less concealed an achievement almost as decisive. The legend has long since been exploded of his counterstroke driving the Prussian Guard into the marshes of St. Gond and deciding the Battle of the Marne. For the German armies to the west were already in retreat, thus compelling a general retirement.

But although Foch's counterstroke was not a decisive factor, his resistance was, for he bore the longest and the severest strain, and if the French centre had broken under the tremendous pressure, the Marne would have been an inevitable defeat and the French enveloping move on the western flank futile to avert disaster. He indeed was the pivot on which Gallieni's manœuvre was based, and those who reproached Gallieni for striking prematurely failed to realize that his counterthrust came only just in time to save the centre breaking under the German pressure.

While Foch's contribution to the victory was by holding fast, this resistance was effected by attack. Perhaps it would be more true to say, by the inspired or — as some of his subordinates thought — insane catchword, "Attaquez." The story has become historic that he reported: "Mon centre cède, ma droite recule, situation excellente, j'attaque." If not true in fact, it was true in spirit. For when his subordinate commanders informed him that they were being borne down by weight of numbers and must fall back unless reënforced, he merely replied with mystical gestures, "Attaquez," and when they hesitated, hurled at them more vehemently than ever the words, "Attaquez, attaquez, attaquez!" So it continued for four days until companies were reduced to a mere score of men led by an N. C. O. At last Eydoux, commander of the 11th Corps, told him that there was no longer hope of an ordered retirement. To which Foch replied, "You say that you cannot hold on and you cannot retreat, so the only thing left is to attack to-morrow morning." When morning came the Germans had gone.

Foch had proved the truth of his saying that "a battle won is a battle which we will not acknowledge to be lost." Nevertheless we have to recognize that Providence was kind to him, that his own opponents retired not because their morale was exhausted, and that but for Gallieni's distant action a will without a living body might have been an inadequate barrier to the Germans.

That "success justifies everything" was Foch's rule, and the successful fact of the Marne soon gave him a still greater opportunity for his will to conquer. The Battle of the Marne was succeeded by the race to the sea, when both armies were seeking to find and turn their enemy's western flank. Unhappily, the Allies were handicapped by the fact that troops of three nations — French, British, and Belgian — took part in this relay race, and in face of a situation changing hourly, Joffre wisely decided that there must be one man on the spot to coördinate the several efforts. He sent Foch to the Nord as "deputy for the commander-in-chief." The novel character of the appointment did not simplify the many difficulties of such a coördinating rôle between allies, but fortunately the very urgency of the danger subdued national scruples. And unfortunately once more Foch's will to conquer found an echo in the spirit of troops who traditionally refused to know when they were beaten. At Ypres, as on the Marne, his refrain, "Attaquez," may not have been translated into fact, but at least its keynote, "Conquer," became fact, because the German aim was foiled. The Allied commanders, who had their feet on the ground, were several times driven to think that a retreat was inevitable, but Foch, with his head in the clouds, refused to listen; the "realists" were overborne by the apparent mystic. Yet to his magical catchword Foch added a shrewd grasp of the right psychological appeal. To the King of the Belgians Foch said that unless he held on to the scrap of Belgian territory which remained he would never be king after the war. And to Sir John French, when at the crisis of the battle, Foch promised that if he would hold on for another twenty-four hours a stated number of French reënforcements would reach him. Twenty-four hours passed and no reënforcements came, but the front still held. Then Foch said, "You have proved that you could hold on for twenty-four hours. Hold on for another twenty-four and this time I give you my word of honor the reënforcements shall arrive." And he added that on the first occasion he had purposely not given his word of honor, because at that time he did not know if and when he could obtain reënforcements. It was in fact a purely moral expedient of the moment, or rather a flash of inspiration.

He was fertile in such expedients, some of which gave a comic interlude to that immortal tragedy. I was told by a highly placed officer how Sir Henry Wilson, a close friend of Foch and Deputy Chief of the British General Staff, was sent several nights successively by Sir John French to argue with Foch upon the need of a retreat. The first time Foch listened, but no more, and thereafter when Henry Wilson appeared Foch immediately said: "*Double Vay*, if you come to talk to me about Ypres it is useless, for such a place is not on my map." And in the upshot Ypres was held and the Channel ports saved. If the attacks by the French reënforcements, ordered by Foch, made little headway, their very audacity gave the German Command the mistaken idea that the Allied strength was greater than in reality. As

Foch himself remarked in retrospect: "One goes forward without knowing the future, without knowing if success will come. But it is necessary to go forward all the same, for in certain cases anything is better than retreat."

When, however, the emergency had passed, and the state of flux had hardened into rigid trench warfare, Foch's reputation suffered a setback, for trench warfare was the reign of material, and Foch found that even will could not conquer the alliance of machine guns and barbed wire.

In 1915 he directed the May and September offensives between Arras and Lens, adjoining the British, but both suffered heavy loss for little gain. The following spring he had a narrow escape from death in a motor accident, but recovered in time to direct the French share of the Somme offensive and to some extent coördinate the whole. The rôle was not easy, for with the British bearing the greater burden he could not well exercise any authority over Haig. Nevertheless, Foch had more than his share of the criticism which arose from this "blood bath," and, unlike his vis-à-vis, lost his command, although the French part of the offensive had been at least more economic than the British. Perhaps, like Hubert Gough in March 1918, the popular disappointment of the moment was used as a pretext for penalizing him on account of earlier and more genuine mistakes. Ill health was the official camouflage for Foch's removal from command — an excuse somewhat amusing in view of the verdict of the doctor who had attended him after his motor accident, that he had "a constitution as robust as a man of thirty."

Joffre gauged the trend of events rightly when at the end of the Somme battle he said, "You are limogé, I shall be limogé, we shall all be limogé," Limoges being the centre to which had been sent the numerous generals dismissed by Joffre himself early in the war. But although Joffre's own fate was to be final, he preserved Foch's services for the army by giving him a theoretical post, to preside over a board of military studies established at Senlis. Early in 1917 Foch was engaged in preparing a plan of defense for the Belfort region in case the Germans should try to come through Switzerland, and in March he was sent to Italy to collaborate with Cadorna the means of common action on that front if the need arose. Saved by a hair's breadth from disgrace, Foch's rehabilitation came sooner than he could have hoped for. When Pétain succeeded Nivelle as commander in chief after the abortive April offensive of 1917, Foch was called to be Chief of the French General Staff, on Pétain's suggestion. This brought Foch back to influence, if not to command, and the Italian disaster in the autumn gave him an opportunity not only to regild his reputation but to impress his personality on the political chiefs of the Allies. While his opposite number in London,

Robertson, was reluctant to dispatch troops from the Western Front, Foch forced his hand by a telegram which announced that the French Government had already ordered four divisions to Italy. And hastening thither himself, he sought to stiffen the resistance by phrases which revived memories of Ypres in 1914. Characteristically, he spoke in parables: "The Italian front was a wall, not of stone, however, but of clay; and when it began to rain on the wall — ?" There was no need to complete the sentence. Similarly, to Cadorna he said: "It is not with water lines that you will defend Italy, but with the breasts of your soldiers."

Foch took part in the Rapallo Conference between the Allied ministers, a meeting which gave birth to the Supreme War Council — the first step toward unity of command, but one which had all the defects of a compromise. Compromise may be the soul and committees the body of politics, but we had still to learn afresh that in war *the man* counts. Foch, Sir Henry Wilson, General Cadorna, and later General Bliss, were appointed the military representatives on this Council, but Foch dropped out for Weygand when it assembled, a move which preserved his influence but diminished the status of the committee. The obvious weakness of this merely advisory body led to its conversion into a military executive committee, with Foch as chairman, which should create and control an interallied general reserve of thirty

divisions. The commanders in chief, Haig and
Pétain, disliked this duality of control, and Haig's
flat statement that he could spare no troops, because
of the extension of his front and the threatening
situation, exploded the futile compromise.

While the various parties were still arguing, the
blow fell on March 21, 1918, and the German tide
swept through the shattered front of Gough's Fifth
Army. The alternative arrangement which the commanders in chief had made between themselves, to
support each other, broke down at an early stage.
To sort out the tangle Lord Milner was sent to
France on March 24 and, after a series of hasty
consultations, a meeting of the French and British
leaders was arranged at Doullens on March 26. Here
Lord Milner proposed that Foch should be given
authority to coördinate the action of the Allied armies,
and gained his point. And it was Haig who suggested that the narrower scope of Foch's authority
in Clemenceau's original draft, "autour d'Amiens,"
should be changed into "sur tout le front." The
words, "sur le front ouest," were finally adopted. On
April 14 this coördination was expanded into command, and Foch was definitely made Commander in
Chief of the Allied Armies. His feeling as to the
future was aptly expressed in his remark to a doubt-
ing Thomas: "Materially, I do not see that victory
is possible. Morally, I am certain that we shall
gain it."

The immediate value of the Doullens decision was that it gave the British commanders an assurance that the situation as a whole, and not merely the French aspect, would be considered, and allowed them to concentrate on the urgent purpose of damming the breach in front of Amiens. Foch certainly stimulated the flow of French reserves thither, but greater claims are unwarranted, for he was hardly in office before the German impetus began to wane in face of the stiffening resistance and the strain on its own communications. But on April 9 Ludendorff launched a fresh blow farther north in the Lys valley, which was threateningly close to the Channel ports. For Foch, subject to pressure from a French Government anxious over the safety of Paris, it was no light step to send French reserves so far north, but he did so, and British critics who complained that they did not come quicker, or more plentifully, did not take full account of his problem.

As in 1914, he set his face against any withdrawal, even to shorten the line as Haig proposed. With a flash of inspiration, or clairvoyance, he declared, "La bataille du nord est finie," when to many observers it looked rather as if the British army was "finie." As usual, he illustrated his opinion by a parable — of the rings made by dropping a stone into water: the first ring large and strong, the succeeding rings gradually smaller and less marked, until they eventually died away altogether. So, first on the Somme and then on the Lys, the force of the German offensive would diminish until the "water" of the battle area became still.

And if he seemed dangerously sparing with reserves, the facts, "which alone count," justified him once more. But a month later his vision, and the French Intelligence Service, failed him when the Germans thrust through the Aisne front and reached the Marne on the fourth day — a dagger pointing at the heart of France. Ludendorff had scored a surprise over Foch, and the latter could not disguise it, for he had insisted that four British divisions which had suffered heavily should go to this "quiet" sector to replace French divisions which he had taken for his reserve.

Foch, however, was as resilient as a rubber ball, full of plans for Allied attacks while others were only wondering how they could stop the Germans. Even before the fresh setback on the Aisne he had issued a "directive" to Haig and Pétain for attacks in front of Amiens and on the Lys in order to free his lateral railway communications. If this design showed his practical belief in his theory of freedom of action, it is also a proof that he had no idea of luring Ludendorff on and allowing him to form vast bulges which Foch could strike in flank — as was a popular view. Similarly, the historian has to recognize that the great counterstroke of July 18, which turned the scales, was not intended as a counterstroke. This legend must share the fate of that about the marshes of St. Gond. Foch's refrain was "Attaquez" and he chanted it so continually that it was almost bound to coincide sometime with a "psychological moment." Thus in the first Battle of the Marne it coincided, on September 10, 1914, with the German retreat, and now in the second Battle of the Marne it coincided with Ludendorff's blow in the air, which had momentarily thrown him off his balance.

For Foch had intended his great counteroffensive, by Mangin's army against the western flank of the Marne bulge, to take place on July 12, in order to anticipate the German attack which he knew Ludendorff was preparing. Foch's motive was prevention, not a respite. His star still watched over him, however; the attack was not ready before Ludendorff struck — and hit the air because of the elastic withdrawal which Pétain had conceived and Gouraud executed. Thus Foch's blow became a true and decisive counterstroke, which definitely wrested the initiative from Ludendorff and gave it to Foch.

At the same time it was Foch's opportunism which seized the opening directly it was offered. He had no intention of "arriving at the station two or three minutes after the train had gone!" While the more cautious Pétain appreciated the strain put upon the defense, Foch had an insight into the way in which the enemy had strained himself.

Mangin has related how Foch, hearing that Pétain had contermanded the attack, promptly exerted himself to have the order cancelled. And later when Pétain would have halted the attack and assumed defensive dispositions, Foch ordered it to continue. Here was the secret of his genius, and the only rule of his strategy: "Success justifies everything, and the secret is, once obtained, to keep the direction of it."

If he had launched Mangin's attack with no more far-reaching aim than to free the Nancy railway, he kept on and kept the initiative. Moreover, his immediate strategy of disengaging his lateral railways was unquestionably the right initial direction, for it gave him freedom of movement for his reserves. Such liberty was essential if his further strategy was to fulfill the law of economy of force and the principle of mobility — for surprise and security. The great surprise won by the British Fourth Army on August 8 in front of Amiens, which for Ludendorff was "the black day of the German army in the history of the war," opened the eyes of Foch to a wider horizon. His critics sometimes assert that Foch won in the end by casting his theories overboard. This was not so. His theories were so ingrained in his mind — and soul — that during four years he had persevered in carrying them into practice without heed to the reality of conditions which made them hopeless. And, because the balance of battle so often turns on the moral element, his "will to conquer" prevailed in certain defensive crises through the very intensity of his belief in the illusion that he was attacking. This faith remained, but hard experience awakened him to the value, if not to the obstacle, of material factors. When, late in 1918, the facts of numerical and material superiority at last made his theories practicable, his deficiencies became assets. For, never having immersed himself in the "business" of siege warfare, his grasp of the eternal principles of strategy enabled him to develop a new offensive method which fulfilled them. Henceforth he beat a tattoo on the German front, a series of rapid blows at different points, each broken off as soon as its initial impetus waned, each so aimed as to pave the way for the next, and all close enough in time and space to react on each other. Thus Ludendorff's power of switching reserves to threatened spots was stopped, as his balance of reserves was drained. If he had cut his loss earlier, — and Germany had been morally strong enough to stand the shock, — he might well have thwarted Foch, but by trying to stand on the Hindenburg Line he lent himself to Foch's strategy. For although on the eve of the Armstice the Allied advance was run to a standstill because supplies could not keep pace, Foch was ready to launch a Franco-American mass in Lorraine against the communications of an enemy who was stripped of reserves.

In this hour of triumph it is Foch's greater glory that in him the mystic gave place to the realist, the lover of battle to the lover of humanity. Realizing that his Armistice terms would give him all the fruits of victory, he sacrificed the ornamental laurels which might, or might not, have come from a continuation of the fight, at the price of more lives.

What place will Foch take in the roll of Great Captains? In the heated enthusiasm of victory he was hailed as the peer almost of Napoleon. A decade later, in the cool light of history, we can see that, as a strategist, the comparison is far-fetched. In will, perhaps, but in art, no. The conditions did not lend themselves to art, for the weight of numbers and the artificial power of defense cramped manœuvre and prevented those dazzling combinations in time and space which are the soul of Napoleon's art. And if Napoleon showed little research for new material factors, Foch showed less, in a more fruitful era. Napoleon, again, bent conditions to his advantage where Foch only seized opportunities — the mark of inspiration, but hardly of sustained genius. Other Napoleonic qualities were lacking: magnetic power over the mass, versatility, grasp of detail, organizing power. If Napoleon had a Berthier, Foch had a Weygand — which was better. It is difficult, and will probably never be possible, to estimate the share of Weygand during that last year, when perfect concord was established between the two. Officers who came into close contact with them had the impression that Weygand thought "Foch" but a little further ahead. And all knew that he brought the organizing power, grasp of detail, and lucidity of expression which were an essential complement to the qualities of his chief. It was the irony of fate that Weygand, who was not a Staff College man, should have been doomed to act as a staff officer throughout the war. That he proved so perfect in his rôle, not only in his work but in self-effacement, was a grim jest at the expense of the man who, endowed with the cavalry spirit, longed to command troops. Fate must have relented at last when it gave him the belated chance to prove in Poland against the Bolsheviks that he had truly the genius for directing great operations.

But however much Foch owed to his collaborator, it is right to recognize that he alone bore the responsibility and that his spirit gave the impetus to the advance of victory. His influence cannot be better expressed than by his own vivid illustration: "War is like this. Here is an inclined plane. An attack is like this ball rolling down it. It goes on gaining momentum and getting faster and faster on condition you do not stop it. If you check it artificially anywhere, you lose your momentum and have to begin all over again." It is true that only the tide of American reënforcements had pushed the ball up the near slope and over the crest, and that the fighting power of the British troops in breaking the Hindenburg Line was vital in maintaining the momentum; but the value of the instruments does not lessen the credit of the guiding hand, which was masterly once the ball had begun rolling and attack had become a fact and not merely a refrain. Moreover, although advanced in years, he showed the elasticity to profit by experience, and by the end of the war had so widened his horizon that it is difficult to estimate how high he might rank among the Great Captains if the war had continued into 1919. The man who before the war emphasized moral at the expense of material factors, in his post-war utterances gave full weight to the change wrought by science and mechanical invention, revealing a profound appreciation alike of the industrialization of war and of the effect of material factors upon the morale of the soldier. Even in the moral sphere his understanding widened, and he shed a new light on the great principle of surprise. "It is necessary, when one has been repulsed for four or five days, not to change one's objectives, but to give them a new form in the guise of a new operation. Only at this price will you get obedience from men. With his natural élan, the French soldier, who loves variety, accepts the idea which appears new to him. The result is that, under a convenient mask, all the forces stealthily converge toward the line, the secret of which has been kept under apparent fluctuations."

As Foch developed a deeper insight into human

nature and the nature of a national war, so he gained a clearer vision of the goal of the war — and he knew when to stop. Thus, if he will rank below Napoleon as a strategist, he may be placed higher as a grand strategist, for of such the security and prosperity of the nation after the war are a better test than brilliancy of manœuvre. In his centenary oration on Napoleon, Foch himself foreshadowed this verdict: "He forgot that a man cannot be God; that beyond the individual there is the nation; that beyond men there is morale; and that war is not the supreme goal, for beyond that there is peace."

Foch himself came through tribulation to triumph not merely because of the turning of the tide of war, but also because his own mental tide had turned, ebbing from the Napoleonic — or, more truly, from his mystical conception of the Napoleonic. Many soldiers study the technique and history of war, a few seek to analyze the moral element, but Foch sought by meditation to grasp the ultimate reality — and in so doing lost hold of earthly reality. Gradually he was brought back from the contemplation of the spirit to knowledge of the facts, from absorption with his own soul to understanding the nation's, from mystic faith in morale to a practical realization that morale depends on *matériel*, and that in war a will can only be effective inside a living body. It may be true that Napoleon forgot more than Foch ever knew. But Napoleon forgot. Foch learned.

ERICH LUDENDORFF
THE ROBOT NAPOLEON

ERICH LUDENDORFF

THE ROBOT NAPOLEON

LIKE the morning mists dispersing as the sun rises farther above the horizon, so has the post-war haze which enshrouded the figure and fame of Erich Ludendorff become clearer in the light of our more fully documented knowledge of the war and our more detached reflection upon its events. In 1919 Ludendorff was the scapegoat of defeat, as execrated by the mass of his countrymen and as belittled by the mass of his victorious foes as Napoleon on the morrow of Waterloo. And in effect, like Napoleon at St. Helena, his vindication has not come about by any personal recovery of power; rather it has been delayed, not assisted, by his post-war activities and utterances. But if it is still too early to estimate Ludendorff's stature in world history, it is possible through the thinning mists to perceive the outline of a figure moulded on a great scale, perhaps the greatest of all among the leaders of the War of 1914–1918, and with the attributes, save of personal magnetism, which may even inspire a second Napoleonic legend. Should this legendary magnification come to pass, the verdict of to-day may be a true mean between the nadir of 1919 and the zenith of to-morrow.

The critic who would appraise the quality of Ludendorff is fortunate in that few great figures have so aptly expressed their powers and limitations alike in their acts. The record of his career is the rating of the man. Born at Kruszevnia, in Prussian Poland, on April 9, 1865, the son of a rural estate agent, his descent from a line of merchants, established in the district since 1600, stamped itself on his character and career. The World War was essentially a middle-class war, and Ludendorff, like his great opponent, Foch, was a symbol of the fact, not only by birth and upbringing, but in mentality.

"Love of the Fatherland and loyalty to the King, together with a clear sense of the obligation upon each individual to live for his duty to family and State — this was the heritage that I took with me from home as my portion in life. My parents were not well-to-do; their devoted efforts brought them no earthly reward. Although very simple and sparing, ours was a happy and harmonious family life. My father and my mother were both of them altogether absorbed in their care for us six children. Thanks be unto our parents for this, before all the world.

"As a young officer, I had to make my way by hard, stand-up fighting. . . . I sat a good deal in my modest subaltern's quarters . . . and read polit-

LUDENDORFF

ical and military history, as well as geographical works. What I had learned as a child bore fruit. I grew proud of my Fatherland, and of its men of mark. I worshiped with glowing fervor the heroic and passionate figure of Bismarck. I gained a clear perception of the workings of our Sovereign House for its Prussia-Germany. The allegiance that I had sworn was transformed within me into a profound sentiment of devotion. As I followed in the footsteps of history . . . I became irresistibly impressed by the decisive importance of the army and of the fleet for our security. At the same time, my survey of life around me enabled me to discern the greatness and significance of the peaceful services rendered by the Fatherland to civilization and to mankind."

In these phrases, obviously sincere, we see the seeds which bore fruit splendid in size but bitter in taste. Here were developed his powers of concentration, but limited horizon, his spiritual devotion to the ideal of kingship combined with the mental arrogance characteristic of the self-made man, his honest belief in the mission of Germany and himself without appreciation of the reaction upon others.

Entering the Prussian army in 1883, his zeal and powers of application brought him out of the ruck of regimental soldiering, and by 1894 on to the first rung of the General-Staff ladder, up which he steadily climbed, even then exerting an influence beyond his years or status. To such a man the German system, where seniority ruled rank but not power, gave great scope. For in the German army the General Staff was truly the power behind the throne, pulling the strings by which their nominal commanders reluctantly but obediently moved. Nay, more, its members were an all-powerful military priesthood, linked by ties of intellectual and professional comradeship. A corps of directors, a society within a society, they were to the German army what the Jesuits at their political zenith were to the Church of Rome. In other armies the able staff officer may be not merely the channel of his commander's orders but their source; nevertheless he is tactful enough, as well as wise enough, to cloak the fact, to consult his superior, and, when giving instructions, to speak in the name of his superior. But in the German army during the war the veil was cast entirely, and a chief of staff would repeatedly take decisions and give orders direct to the chiefs of staff of lower units without mention of or reference to the respective commanders. Thus it is that in German war histories any reference to a particular army or corps is often phrased significantly: ". . . Army; Commander, General X (Chief of Staff, Colonel Y)."

In the Operations Branch Ludendorff came in close and inspiring contact with Graf von Schlieffen, creator of the German war plan, and when in 1908 Ludendorff became head of the Aufmarschabteilung, he strove to ensure the material conditions requisite for the success of this plan. He it was who worked out the last important German Army Bill before the war, which was passed by the Reichstag in 1913; but while most of his technical reforms were carried through, his proposal for three new army corps was dropped by the Minister of War. To his inconvenient insistence on this point may be traced his second brief return to regimental duty — he had been a company commander from 1898–1900. His appointment to command the 39th Fusilier Regiment at Düsseldorf was virtually a demotion, and even his early advancement to command a brigade at Strassburg hardly compensated for his former influence. However, three months later the outbreak of war came to his rescue, and he took up his war position as Quartermaster-General of Bülow's Second Army. But, like Napoleon at Toulon, fortune intervened to take him from his assigned duty and give him the chance of winning an early distinction which vitally influenced his career.

The attack on Liége was being made by a specially detached force under General von Emmich, and Ludendorff was sent to watch this and ensure its liaison with Bülow's Second Army. In the first attack four of the five German brigades were repulsed, while the other, losing its commander, was held up. General Ludendorff arrived on the spot at this critical moment, took charge of this last brigade, the 14th, and through his energy, aided by a mistaken withdrawal of some of the Belgian troops, gained the heights commanding Liége after an all-night street battle, and entered the town early in the morning, August 8, 1914. This penetration and Ludendorff's driving force in arranging a fresh siege army paved the way for the complete capture of the fortress. For this feat he received the order Pour le Mérite, and a fuller reward soon followed.

While the German armies were advancing through Belgium, their protective army in East Prussia was menaced by an invasion which the Russians had hurriedly launched to ease the pressure on their French allies. Pressed heavily in front by Rennenkampf's army, the German commander, Prittwitz, momentarily lost his head on hearing that another army under Samsonov had crossed the southern frontier of East Prussia in his rear. In a telephone message he spoke of falling back behind the Vistula, whereupon the Chief of the German General Staff, Moltke, instantly superseded him by a retired general, Hindenburg, to whom Ludendorff was appointed as chief of staff. Ludendorff reached supreme headquarters at Coblenz on August 22, and after the situation in the East had been explained to him, without waiting for Hindenburg, who joined the train at Hanover, he telegraphed orders for the first of a series of moves which were to culminate in a new Cannæ — the victory of Tannenberg. It is just to recognize that their execution was vitally facilitated by steps already initiated by Colonel Hoffmann, of Prittwitz's staff.

Let us pause, however, for a moment to contemplate this charming and amusing picture of the German system of command. The comparatively young staff officer — for Ludendorff was barely forty-nine — chosen first, and his nominal commander second, as if to say, "Ludendorff is the man we want to save the situation in the East; whom shall we give him as a figurehead?" The staff officer summoned to take counsel with the Supreme Command, his nominal commander waiting unclaimed in the "lost property office" at Hanover. The staff officer forming the plan, telegraphing *his* orders, and then collecting Hindenburg, like part of his baggage, en route to his destination !

Ludendorff concentrated some six divisions against Samsonov's left wing. These might have sufficed to dislocate but not to crush the Russian advance. Finding, however, that Rennenkampf was slow to push forward, Ludendorff took the calculated risk of withdrawing the bulk of the German troops from that front and rushed them back against Samsonov's right wing. This daring move was aided by the absence of communication between the Russian commanders and by their folly in sending unciphered wireless orders which the Germans could read. By this converging manœuvre, Samsonov's flanks were enveloped and one so badly crushed by François (German 1st Corps) that Samsonov's centre was cut off, and his army practically annihilated. Then, receiving a reënforcement of two fresh army corps, the Germans turned on the dilatory Rennenkampf and drove him out of East Prussia. But a fresh danger arose, which Ludendorff averted by a truly Napoleonic manœuvre, one which, if less spectacular in result than Tannenberg, is perhaps the finest example of his art as well as one of the classic masterpieces of all military history.

The Russians had compensated Tannenberg by great victories in Southern Poland, and to relieve their Austrian allies, the bulk of the German forces in East Prussia were formed into a new Ninth Army, which joined in a combined advance from the Cracow area toward Warsaw. The Russians, however, were nearing the full tide of their mobilized strength, and not only threw back the Austro-Germans, but planned a counterinvasion of Silesia, employing a phalanx of seven armies — three in the van and two protecting each flank. For the first and last time in the war the legendary Russian steam-roller got up steam, and for the first and last time also a vital part of German territory was endangered.

Faced with the emergency, Falkenhayn, Moltke's successor, placed the whole Eastern Front under Hindenburg-Ludendorff, but would spare no extra forces to ensure success to the masterly counterstroke which Ludendorff's brain had conceived, although on the West he left veteran troops to lie idle in Lorraine while he sacrificed raw masses in his vain efforts to break through at Ypres. Ludendorff's plan was based on the lateral railways inside the German frontier. The Ninth Army, retreating in the Cracow direction before advancing Russians, slowed them down by a systematic destruction of all communications; and itself, on withdrawing to the frontier, was first switched northward and next thrust southeast up the Vistula against the joint between the two Russian armies guarding this flank. The wedge, driven in by Ludendorff's mallet, split the two armies, forced one back on Warsaw and nearly "Tannenberged" the other. If the wedge lacked the reënforcement necessary for decisive tactical success and was itself imperiled, this Lodz manœuvre achieved its strategic object of dislocating the Russian advance. It will live as a classic example of how a small force, by using its mobility to strike at a vital point, can paralyze a vastly larger army. When the greater chance had gone, four fresh German army corps arrived a week later.

The real story of 1915 on the German side is the moral tug-of-war between Falkenhayn and Ludendorff. The former, unwillingly dissuaded from a renewed attempt to force the Allied trench-barrier, made up his mind to stand on the defensive in the West, but seemingly without any clear strategic purpose. His feeling that the war must ultimately be decided in the West led him to distrust the value, as he doubted the possibility, of a decision against Russia. His was a strategy of compromise, doling out reserves reluctantly to ward off danger to his Austrian allies, and compelled to continue the dole because a mere defensive would not suffice and a partial offensive could find no secure halting place. Ludendorff, in contrast, had his vision fixed on a definite goal, whether right or wrong, and from now on pressed unceasingly for a whole-hearted effort to wipe Russia off the military slate. In the conflict of wills between these two men lies the clue to the resultant strategy of Germany — highly effective, yet not decisive.

Ludendorff, in East Prussia, was little more than a spectator of the first phase of the 1915 campaign, which opened in May with Mackensen's breakthrough on the Dunajec between Tarnow and Gorlice, and in a few weeks rolled the Russian armies back to Lemberg. Tactically unlimited, its strategical object was at first limited to relieving the pressure on the Austrians, but its astonishing success and immense captures made it difficult to call a halt, and thereafter Falkenhayn was towed in the wake of the machine he had released, a defective yet too effective brake on its progress. He changed the direction — hitherto eastward — up toward the north, ordering Hindenburg at the same time to strike southeast. Ludendorff disliked the plan as being too much of a frontal attack; the closing-in of the two wings might squeeze the Russians, but would not cut them off. His own plan was a wide enveloping movement round the northern flank near the Baltic, through Kovno and Vilna, toward the Russian rear communications, but Falkenhayn refused, shrinking both from its boldness and from its demand upon his reserves. The upshot fulfilled Ludendorff's anticipation — the Grand Duke Nicholas extricated his bruised forces from the overshallow salient before Falkenhayn's shears could close upon them. Thereupon Falkenhayn broke off large-scale operations, but gave Ludendorff a tardy permission to attempt his Vilna manœuvre with such meagre resources as he had. Ludendorff launched it on September 9, the armies of Below and Eichhorn forming two great horns which gored their way into the northern sector of the Russian front, the one east toward Dvinsk and the other southeast toward Vilna. The Russians were driven back in divergent directions, and the German cavalry, issuing from between the horns, pressed forward until they far overlapped Vilna and drew near the Minsk railway — a vital artery of communication with the heart of Russia. But the German strength was slender, the Russians free to concentrate against this isolated menace, and in face of the stiffening resistance Ludendorff took the wise course of suspending operations.

The crux of the situation was that the Russian armies
had been allowed — by Falkenhayn — to draw back
almost out of the net before the long-delayed Vilna
manœuvre was sanctioned; the degree of success
attained by such weak forces was proof of the
practicability of the manœuvre and of Ludendorff's
claim that such a blow, delivered in force while the
Russians were deeply enmeshed in the Polish salient,
might have annihilated the military power of Russia.
As it was, although crippled, she was able to delay
the concentration of Germany's strength in the West
for a further two years. Falkenhayn's cautious
attrition strategy was to prove the more hazardous
gamble, and paved the way for Germany's bankruptcy.

In 1916 Falkenhayn carried his idea of attrition
into the tactical sphere, and at Verdun fulfilled his
long-cherished aim of a Western offensive. But,
while this deliberate method pursued its laborious
course, the reprieved Russian army made, through
Brusilov, a flickering effort which had great strategic
consequences. The threatened collapse of the Austrians compelled Falkenhayn to withdraw troops
from the West and give up his intended counterstroke
against the British attack on the Somme, sealed the
failure of Verdun, and led to the entry of Rumania.
Falkenhayn fell from power, having wrecked his
country's fortunes by a refusal to take calculated
risks. On August 29, 1916, Hindenburg was called

to be Chief of General Staff, and Ludendorff, as First Quartermaster-General, became the directing brain of Germany's war effort henceforward. He had to take over a concern which, if not bankrupt, was in serious difficulties, and the sombre spirit in which he entered upon his new rôle was a true reflection of the facts. That he was not called to it earlier was the Allies' salvation — such may be the verdict of history. While he set on foot a complete programme for the reorganization and expansion of German man-power, munitions, and supplies, he had to stave off the imminent military dangers. Adopting against Rumania the plan already framed by Falkenhayn, he put his own brain and driving force into its coördination and execution by the two converging armies of Mackensen and Falkenhayn.

Rumania's entry into the war had come at an awkward moment for the enemy, and her invasion of Transylvania threatened danger to the heart of Austria-Hungary, denuded of troops. But the Rumanian army, strong in numbers, was weak in equipment and organization, and its slow advance gave the enemy command breathing space to scrape together forces for a swift countermove. This was facilitated by the lie of Rumania's territory, forming an L reversed, with the lower section — Wallachia — sandwiched between Transylvania to the north and Bulgaria to the south. With better leadership on her own part, or less able opponents, she might not have suffered from this geographical situation, for as the mountain barrier of the Carpathians separated her from Transylvania, so the Danube shielded all her territory, except the Dobruja, from Bulgaria.

While Falkenhayn's force concentrated in Transylvania, a Bulgarian army with German stiffening — under Mackensen — invaded Rumania's back yard, the Dobruja. This was a shrewd moral stroke, for the automatic strategic effect was to draw away the Rumanian reserves intended to support the Transylvanian offensive, and so check its progress for want of nourishment.

Falkenhayn moved next, and his counteroffensive threw back the Rumanian main armies and nearly penetrated the Carpathian passes on their heels. Foiled here, he swung farther south and, although at first checked, a concentrated last-minute effort broke through to the Wallachian plain on November 17, a few days before the passes were blocked by the winter snows.

It was the signal for the next move in Ludendorff's combination. Mackensen switched the bulk of his force back from the Dobruja westward, forced the crossing of the Danube close to Bucharest on November 23, and thus turned the flank of the Rumanian armies opposing Falkenhayn. Under the converging pressure of the two German "fists," the Rumanian armies were driven back and penned in the northern corner of their territory. By the end of December the swift German strategy had crippled their new foe and gained possession of the bulk of Rumania, with its wheat and oil. This brief campaign revealed the fallacy of mere numbers, and the much-abused saying of Napoleon the Emperor, that God is on the side of the big battalions, received yet another historical contradiction from Alexander's — and Bonaparte's — principle that real strength lies in quality and mobility rather than quantity.

Ludendorff could now turn his energy to the problem of relieving the pressure on his Western Front.

To meet the renewal of the Franco-British Somme offensive, which he foresaw in the spring, he had a new line of defense, of great artificial strength, built across the chord of the arc Lens-Noyon-Rheims. Then, after devastating the whole area inside the arc, he began a methodical withdrawal, by stages, to the new line, called by the Germans the "Siegfried," and by the Allies the "Hindenburg" line. A consummate manœuvre, if brutal in application, the giving up of territory revealed Ludendorff's moral courage, and it dislocated the Allies' plans.

But Ludendorff still needed time for his home programme to mature, and although opposed to such a step hitherto, he yielded to the pleas of the naval authorities for an "unlimited" submarine campaign, and their promise that it would be decisive. If his military horizon perhaps limited the fullness of his political view, it is but just to recognize certain facts :

he fully realized that the step meant America's entry, and accepted it as the lesser of two evils, with the hope, but no more, of winning in the race between Germany's inevitable exhaustion and America's effective influence on the struggle. The maritime and economic history of 1917–1918 bears witness that his was no blind gamble. There is more accuracy in the criticism that Ludendorff was too much a soldier to realize the consequences of a peace by defeat; he saw Germany as a body of simple soldiers rather than as a complex industrial nation, and expected of her the same willingness to achieve victory or die fighting in the attempt. He was given immense power, but wanted all — not to be dictator, but to dictate to the politicians. In July 1917 he secured the resignation of the Chancellor, but not the election of his own nominee, and thenceforth bickering was continual, to the detriment of solidarity and national morale. He advocated universal conscription, industrial as well as military, a measure of justice which the fighting men of all nations desired, but as Germany's collapse began in the rear its nonadoption can hardly be blamed for defeat. But if he did not get all he wanted from the home front, the collapse of the Russians was a compensation he hardly anticipated, and he might well regard the Russian Revolution as an augury, for 1918, that "Fortune favors the brave."

Caporetto was another; for although he had decided on a blow to lame Italy as being essential to

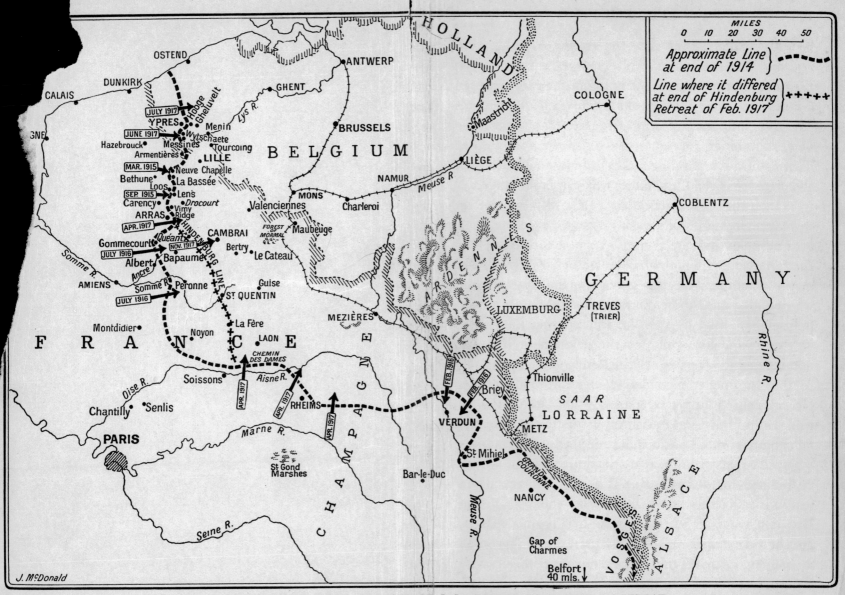

MILES
0 10 20 30 40 50

Approximate Line
at end of 1914

Line where it differed
at end of Hindenburg
Retreat of Feb. 1917

HOLLAND

OSTEND

CALAIS

GNE

DUNKIRK

ANTWERP

GHENT

JULY 1917

YPRES Hooge Gheluvelt
        Menin

JUNE 1917 Wytschaete
Hazebrouck Messines Tourcoing

Armentières

MAR. 1915 LILLE
            Neuve Chapelle
Bethune   La Bassée
    Loos
SEP. 1915   Lens
Carency   Drocourt
ARRAS Vimy
       Ridge

APR. 1917

Gommecourt Quéant CAMBRAI
JULY 1916 NOV. 1917 Bertry
Albert Bapaume   Le Cateau
  Ancre
AMIENS Somme R.
         Peronne Guise
JULY 1916   ST QUENTIN

Montdidier   La Fère
        Noyon
            LAON
                CHEMIN
                DES DAMES
Soissons   Aisne R.
APR. 1917
        APR. 1917 RHEIMS

Chantilly Senlis

PARIS

Marne R.

St Gond
Marshes   Bar-le-Duc

Seine R.

BELGIUM

BRUSSELS

LIÈGE

NAMUR

MONS
Charleroi

Valenciennes

FOREST
OF
MORMAL
Maubeuge

MEZIÈRES

CHAMPAGNE

Lys R.

Maastricht

Meuse R.

A R D E N N E S

LUXEMBURG

FEB. 1916

Thionville
FEB. 1916 Briey
VERDUN

METZ

St Mihiel GRAND DE
           COURONNE

NANCY

Gap of
Charmes

Belfort
40 mls.

COLOGNE

COBLENTZ

G E R M A N Y

TREVES
(TRIER)

SAAR
LORRAINE

Rhine R.

V O S G E S

A L S A C E

Oise R.

Meuse R.

J. McDonald

THE WESTERN FRONT FROM THE END OF 1914 TO THE HINDENBURG RETREAT

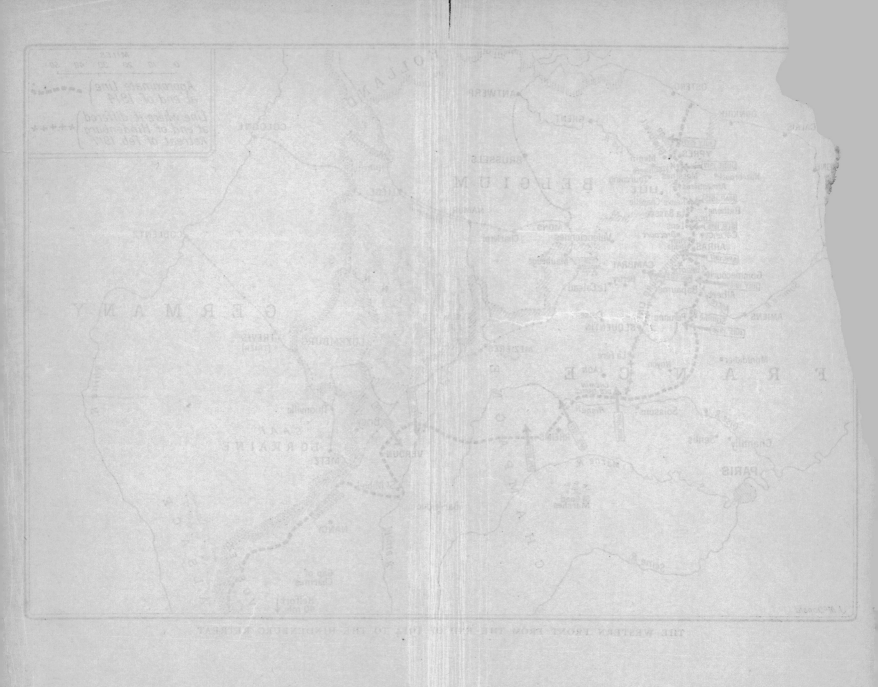

THE WESTERN FRONT FROM THE END OF 1914 TO THE HINDENBURG RETREAT.

encourage the war-weary Austrians, he could only spare six divisions, and skillfully as the point for the thrust had been chosen, it was so light that the Italians' utter collapse was beyond all expectation. There are few more remarkable feats in the history of war than the use Ludendorff made in 1917, between July and October, of this slender general reserve of six divisions — first, to dislocate Russia's last offensive, next in the coup against Riga, and then at Caporetto. The Italian frontier province of Venezia formed a "tongue" pointing toward Austria and flanked on the south by the Adriatic, and on the east and north by the Julian and Carnic Alps, beyond which lay the Austrian Trentino. The six German divisions with nine Austrian formed the Fourteenth German Army under Otto von Below, and were to climb the mountain barrier at the tip of the tongue, while Boroevic's two Austrian armies were to advance along the strip of lower ground near the Adriatic shore. The difficulties of organizing and deploying an attack in the mountains were overcome and on October 24, 1917, the blow was launched. It was pushed deep down the western slopes of the mountains and in four days reached Udine, until then the Italian General Headquarters, imperiling the Italian forces to both north and south.

Not the least significant feature of this offensive was that it was prepared not by an artillery but by a moral bombardment. Propaganda had been exploited for months as a means of sapping the Italian discipline and will to resist. Cadorna, the Italian commander, had failed alike to counteract this demoralization and to guard against the military attack of which he had ample warning.

But its effect seems also to have surprised Ludendorff, who with his slender forces had not calculated on such distant objectives as were now within reach. His belated attempt to switch troops from the left wing to the right for a downward thrust against the Italian rear, and thus make the victory strategically decisive, was foiled by inadequate rail communications, and left Austria with a more difficult front to hold when the Italian army recovered from its temporary concussion. Caporetto is a landmark in Ludendorff's career, for it is the first time, but not the last, when his strategic conception is drawn in the wake of his tactical plan, instead of guiding it.

With the release of the German forces from the Russian front, Ludendorff was now ready for his supreme effort to win the war in the West before Germany's exhaustion and America's forces turned the scales. To secure the rear of his offensive, a definite peace was won from the Bolshevik Government by a military demonstration, and also forced on Rumania. And to secure if possible the economic base of his offensive the Ukraine was occupied for its wheat supplies. Ludendorff had given proof of his tactical originality by the elastic method of

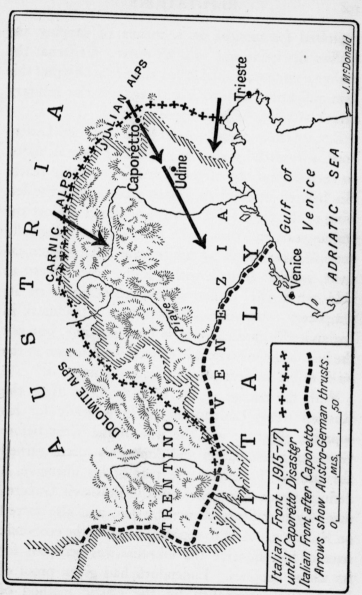

CAPORETTO

diluted defense, which had discomfited the British at Ypres and Passchendaele, and now in the preparation of his offensive his tactical genius and organization were at the highest level in their research for surprise and infiltration. His sole glaring failure was in his inability, characteristic of his type, to realize in time the potentialities of any totally new weapon, such as the tank. Not until August 1918 would he allow the manufacture of tanks to be put in the "urgent" class of war material with aircraft and submarines. By grim coincidence it was the month when the massed British tanks struck a blow on the Somme which Ludendorff later came to recognize as the fatal turning point of the war's crisis.

Lacking tanks, Ludendorff had to fall back on an improved use of existing methods in his attempt, in the spring of 1918, to force the trench deadlock in France. His solution was a compound of wider frontages of attack, the prompt infusion of reserves, new infantry tactics, and an artillery preparation which should be short enough to ensure surprise yet compensate its brevity by its intensity. The keynote of the new infantry tactics was infiltration and manœuvre by the little dispersed groups of automatic-rifle men and machine-gunners. Instead of thick lines breaking themselves against the defender's posts, the groups penetrated between and pushed rapidly onward, while the islets of resistance, cut off from help by the advancing flood, were outflanked and reduced by fresh troops from the reserve. Instead of the old massed blow, the object was rather the filtering of the attacking force into the enemy's defensive system, crumbling it away. The concentration of troops served as a reservoir for supplying the multiple jets, not as a wave to sweep over the defense. For surprise, the masses of artillery were brought up close to the front line in concealment, their ranges obtained by methods which did away with preliminary registration, and the surprise effect of the short five hours' bombardment was increased by a lavish use of gas and smoke shell. The attacking divisions were only brought up during the night previous to the assault, and a continuous leap-frogging of reserve divisions through the exhausted leading divisions maintained the momentum of the advance.

This wealth of tactical invention is evidence of Ludendorff's breadth of mind and receptiveness — perhaps more than of his originality. For, as Ludendorff was the brain of Hindenburg, so, if in a less degree, he himself owed much to certain brilliant assistants. The developments in artillery tactics and most of the decisive artillery battle concentrations, not only in 1918 but during earlier years, were devised by Colonel Bruchmüller, who, coming back from the retired list, proved himself the greatest artillery expert of the war, called in as consultant to any important operation wherever it might be.

Similarly, the textbooks of the new infantry and combined tactics were drawn up by Captain Geyer and other gifted and original-minded young men. In the design of operations Ludendorff owed much to the strategical brains of Lieutenant-Colonel Hoffmann, while he was on the Eastern Front, and of Lieutenant-Colonel Wetzell, when he came to the Supreme Command. Whereas the other arts are, at their height, individual, the art of war is essentially orchestral. To vary the comparison, it may be said of it more expressively than politely that "large fleas have little fleas upon their backs to bite 'em, and little fleas have lesser fleas, and so ad infinitum."

Ludendorff's next problem was to decide his initial direction of attack. The sector between Arras and St. Quentin was chosen, on the western face of the huge salient formed by the German front in France. The choice was governed by tactical reasons — this sector was the Allies' weakest point and the ground offered fewer difficulties than elsewhere — although Ludendorff had in mind the possibility of separating the British and French armies and driving the first back against the Channel coast, too closely penned in to evade the blows. The tactical bias, however, was to have vital results, leading the Germans to change direction and dissipate their strength, owing to their principle of taking the line of least resistance. To this blow toward the Somme and Amiens, the code name "Michael" was given, and Ludendorff also made preparations for successive attacks at other points, which besides being in readiness for the future helped to mystify the Allies. Three points were on the British front and one on the French — "Mars," to follow immediately after "Michael," and immediately north of it, between Arras and Lens, "St. George I" against the Lys sector, "St. George II" against Ypres, and "Blücher" in Champagne. The Michael opening move was to be made on the forty-seven-mile front, Arras-St. Quentin-La Fère, but its main force was intended to be exerted north of the central axis formed by the Somme River, and after breaking through was to wheel northwest and press the British army against the coast, while the river guarded the flank of the wheeling attack.

The blow was launched on March 21, and while it broke through completely south of the Somme, where the defense was thinnest, it was held up near Arras, a check which reacted on all the attack north of the river and on the intended Mars sequel. As a result, on March 23 Ludendorff abandoned his original idea, and directed his main advance toward Amiens. By March 27 the advance had penetrated nearly forty miles, and three days later the German flood was almost lapping the outworks of Amiens. But their route had led the Germans across the desert of the old Somme battlefields of 1916, a brake on communications and supply, and to an area where the French, although tardy, could most easily support their hard-pressed allies. The emergency appointment of Foch on March 26 to coördinate the Allied operations helped to cement the already hardening resistance. Thus on April 9 Ludendorff launched his St. George I attack on the Lys, and its astonishing success against a weakened front led him to convert it into a major effort. The British were desperately close to the sea, but once again their resistance stopped the German tide, just short of the important railway junction of Hazebrouck. Now at last the swelling volume of American reënforcements was promising early relief to the Allies. For Germany the sands were running out and, realizing this, Ludendorff launched his Blücher attack, between Soissons and Rheims, on May 27. Falling by surprise with forty divisions against seven, on a thirty-mile front, it swept over the Aisne and reached the Marne on May 30, where its impetus died away. Blocked frontally by the river, an attempt was made to push west, but it failed in face of Allied resistance, notable for the appearance and counterattack of American divisions at Château-Thierry.

Ludendorff had now created three huge bulges in the Allied front, and his next essay was to pinch out the Compiègne tongue between the Amiens and Marne bulges. But this time there was no surprise, and the blow on the west of the tongue, June 9, was

too late to coincide with the pressure on the east.
A month's pause followed.   Ludendorff was anxious
to strike his long-cherished decisive blow against the
British in Belgium, but he considered that their
reserves here were still too strong, and so again decided to take the line of least resistance, hoping that
a heavy blow in the south would draw off the British.
He had failed to pinch out the Compiègne tongue
on the west of his Marne bulge; he was now to
attempt the same method on the east, by a two-
handed punch on either side of Rheims.   But he
needed an interval for rest and preparation, and the
delay was fatal, giving the British and French time
to recuperate, and the Americans to gather strength.
Moreover, he again lacked the essential element of
surprise, and was foiled also by the new method of
elastic defense adopted by the French.   His failure
on July 15 was followed by the Allied riposte on July
18 — the tide had definitely turned.   The shadow of
Caporetto had hung over his strategy throughout the
1918 campaign.

If, wiser than the British Command at Passchendaele, he chose his sectors of attack in the light of
tactical condition, he failed in following tactical success — the line of least resistance — at the expense
of the strategical goal.   From the experience of the
vain Allied attacks he had drawn the deduction that
"tactics had to be considered before purely strategical objects, which it is futile to pursue unless tactical

success is impossible." Presumably he hoped by firm control to guide these tactical movements to a strategic destination. If so, the story of the St. Quentin, Lys, and Champagne offensives — in March, April, and May 1918 — is the record of his failure. The tactical success of his own blows was his undoing. Yielding to their influence, he pressed each too far and too long, so using up his own reserves and causing an undue interval before the next blow. He had driven in three great wedges, but none severed a vital artery, and the Germans were left with an extended and indented front which invited flanking counterstrokes.

How Foch accepted the invitation has been told in another memoir. In the surprise breach on August 8 of the German lines before Amiens by the British Fourth Army, Ludendorff first recognized the writing on the wall, and the vigor of his arguments for a peace move was redoubled by the collapse of Bulgaria and the beginning of Foch's general offensive. In this crisis Ludendorff's fault seems to have been a duality between his rôle as director of the nation and as a military leader. As the first, he was too slow to see the necessity for peace; as the second, too quick. And having treated the politicians as pawns, they were unfitted to respond when he suddenly took them into his confidence, and their awakening to reality found a prompt echo in a general moral collapse of the "home front." Too late he sought

to rally them to the possibility of a successful defense
of the frontier as a means to better peace terms, and,
fallen into discredit, he resigned on October 6. With
the helmsman gone, the derelict drifted for five weeks,
sinking ever lower in the water, until the end came.

Brilliant as was the Ludendorff of 1918 in the
tactical field, the contrast between his strategy in the
last year and that on the Eastern Front is so pronounced that it cannot be explained merely by the
different conditions and severer opposition. The
difference is one of motive more than results, between
far-sight and short-sight. A knowledge of history
and of human nature may supply the truest explanation, that he was feeling the strain of directing so
many vast operations; for the campaign leaves the
impression that he had neither his former clearness
as to the goal, nor quite the same grip on the changing
situation. He was, in fact, Napoleon at Waterloo.
Over his post-war activities — his inglorious association with various reactionary intrigues, his superficial leadership of the German Fascists, and his
quarrel with Prince Rupprecht of Bavaria — it is
fairest to pass the sponge, for few men shine in their
St. Helena, and his incapacity to understand the
political and civilian outlook was manifest before.
He was essentially the product of his country and
of his age, which had been moulded by the industrial
revolution and nineteenth-century philosophy. For

half a century Germany had been converting herself
into a gigantic war machine, and in Ludendorff she
at least found the one mechanized brain capable of
controlling this scientific monster, which in size alone
was too vast to be human. It is thus absurd to
deprecate Ludendorff because he lacked the personal
magnetism and human understanding of earlier Great
Captains — a specialist and materialist age, and a
war where numbers had swamped the human element,
required and could only evolve the pattern of a great
captain who was a thinking Robot, driven by an
immense power of concentration which precluded a
wider outlook. Most of the leaders were swept up
by the machine and carried helplessly away, but
Ludendorff mastered it for long enough to impress a
Napoleonic stamp on the otherwise incoherent process of mechanical slaughter politely termed "attrition." On Ludendorff the verdict of history may
well be that he was the Robot Napoleon.

PÉTAIN

MILITARY ECONOMIST

PÉTAIN

MILITARY ECONOMIST: THE BLEND OF FABIUS AND CARNOT

RARELY has history offered such a conjunction of opposites as in the two great French leaders of the later part of the World War. The contrast is a strong argument for the influence of natal environment. For while Foch, the Pyrenean, mingled the fire and imagination of the Meridional with the mysticism and tough fibre of the mountain people, Pétain typified the clear, hard-headed business sense of the Nord. And if hasty critics frequently termed Foch "insane," the severest critic of Pétain could only say that he regarded war with a sanity of outlook too extreme for him to plumb the depths or scale the heights in that "impassioned drama." The characteristics of the two, and the contrast between them, were illustrated to me with truth and brevity by a distinguished French officer who, taking a pencil and paper, drew this simple diagram : —

Foch
Pétain

While Foch is surrounded by an atmosphere of romance, himself a corporal mystery and the very inspiration of legend, the only romantic things about Pétain are his Christian names and eighteen months of his career.

Henri Philippe Benoni Omer Joseph Pétain was born on May 24, 1856 at Cauchy la Tour in the Pas de Calais. Thus in 1914 he was already fifty-eight years of age and — here comes another contrast with Foch — was only a colonel, commanding the 33rd Regiment of Infantry at Arras. Whereas the one had been a focus of attention for nearly twenty years, of international reputation as one of the leaders of French military thought, the other seemed on the point of passing from comparative obscurity into definite retirement. It was fortunate for France that the outbreak of war saved him for her service; she could better have spared any other leader, — a bold statement, yet true, — for without him she might never have survived 1917. Even a Foch would have been more likely to hasten than to check this ruin.

How was it that so able a soldier had risen so slowly? Probably because he retained his sanity when most of the French leaders were obsessed with delusions about the *offensive à outrance*. Anything more repellent to their pre-war outlook than the theory and practice of Pétain from 1915 onward cannot be conceived. Added to the distrust which is the lot of all who stand against the stream, he never hesitated to express views which might be

PÉTAIN

unpalatable to authority. It is the cause and the explanation why in every army during peace many of the ablest and most original minds leave the service as colonels, or earlier. And Pétain, like many reserved men, had an unconscious brusqueness of manner which was a shield for shyness. Even in appearance he was the antithesis of Foch, who when debating important questions with Pétain gave observers the impression of a gamecock pecking furiously — his arguments had a muscular accompaniment — at a graven statue. For Pétain's commanding height and bulk, allied to an inhuman calm, gave him a statuesque majesty. Perhaps not only birthplace but school environment accentuated the difference, for whereas Foch was a product of the semicivil Polytechnique, Pétain was a St. Cyrien, and the Spartan discipline of St. Cyr rarely fails to leave its impression on those who pass through it — a harder school even than Sandhurst or West Point. Subsequently he passed through the École de Guerre, and in 1902 became an instructor at the Châlons small-arms school, afterward being appointed an assistant professor at the École de Guerre, where he took the course in infantry tactics. Clearness and common sense distinguished his lectures, and in an era when the moral factors were theoretically pressed to the pitch of absurdity, he stressed the importance of the material factors, especially artillery.

Although still a colonel when war broke out, he

had acting command of a brigade which formed part of Lanrezac's Fifth Army at the Battle of Charleroi. He handled this so well in checking the German advance across the Meuse — which threatened to cut off this exposed flank army — that at the end of the great retreat, when so many commanders were dismissed, he was promoted to command the 6th Infantry Division. Plunged immediately into the Battle of the Marne, his successful attack on Montceau-les-Provins and beyond contributed to the early success of the Fifth Army, now under Franchet d'Espérey, which was the only army to score a tactical victory in that strategically decisive battle. By driving back the right of Bülow's Second Army (German) it combined with other factors to cause the German order for a general retreat. The attack of Pétain's division was notable for the strong and well-planned artillery preparation which foreshadowed the method universally adopted later in trench warfare. Pétain's reward came early, for in October he was advanced to command of the 33rd Army Corps, which, now that the front was being prolonged to the sea, held the sector near Arras. From command of a regiment to command of an army corps in two months was a record, and if old in years he proved that his mind was still young and elastic by being almost the first to grasp the change brought about by siege conditions. If there was no scope for the artist there was urgent demand for the organizer, and to Pétain must be given the credit of being the first to apply "big business" methods to the conduct of the new warfare.

The French Command planned to deliver their first large-scale attack of 1915 in this sector, under the direction of Foch. It was to be made by the four army corps of d'Urbal's Tenth Army, and Pétain's corps was at the left centre near Carency. He had organized the attack in minute detail, personally visiting every battery and watching each fire one round in order to see that it had registered on the exact target laid down in the plan. Everywhere he questioned the regimental officers and N. C. O.'s to make sure that they were clear as to their rôle. If such immersion in detail violated the canons of command and would certainly have been anathema to a Foch, it paid in a war where the general was reduced to the rôle of a machine-tender.

The attack was launched on May 9, 1915. While the other corps were quickly held up, with murderous losses, Pétain's men swept through the German defenses and on for three miles without a check, the infantry carrying conspicuous markers to enable the artillery to follow their progress. They gained the Vimy Ridge and for a few hours it seemed that the whole German front might crumble. Twenty miles away, at Lille, the German Army Group headquarters were even taking steps for a possible hasty removal. But the French Higher Command failed to exploit the chance and for want of reënforcements the gap was closed. By the afternoon German counterattacks began a pressure which regained part of the lost ground.

In recognition of his personal success, Pétain, next month, was given command of the Second Army and entrusted with the main share of the September offensive in Champagne, on which vast hopes were pinned. The eternal optimists who prevailed in every army had a vision of the Germans being thrown back over the distant French frontier.

This time, however, Pétain's methodical instincts led him too far, for the supreme and essential asset of surprise was thrown away by a preliminary bombardment which lasted for three days and nights. The method paid up to a point, for the first German positions were quickly overrun and without severe loss, but the ample warning enabled the Germans to bring up reserves and their second position defied the attack. Worse still the "bag" of 25,000 prisoners was far more than offset by the appalling later losses, due to the folly of the French Higher Command in pressing the attack for days after hope had vanished. The lesson was not lost on Pétain, who had already stopped his attack in disregard of de Castelnau's orders, and his report on the battle became the textbook of the new trench-warfare doctrine.

The immortal crisis of Verdun in the spring of 1916 converted his military reputation into popular fame, and if he had been ambitious would have brought him much more. When the German advance began on February 21 it took by surprise a French Higher Command which had neglected the warnings of the storm, and the fact that, unlike previous offensives, it swelled in violence from a comparatively gentle start, hid the degree of the danger. Only on February 24 did Joffre's headquarters at Chantilly awake to the grave menace, and late that night de Castelnau departed for Verdun to examine the situation. At his instigation, before leaving, Pétain was summoned to Chantilly and placed by Joffre in charge of the defense of Verdun. The interview was characteristic of these two imperturbable men, Joffre concluding with the remark, "Well, my friend, now you are easy in your mind." The apparent absurdity meant that Joffre knew his man.

Pétain's first problem was not so much defense as supply. The German heavy guns had closed all avenues except one light railway and the Bar-le-Duc–Verdun road. To push up troops was no use unless they could be fed and supplied with ammunition. The road was already cracking under the strain of incessant transport, and so 8000 Pioneers and Terri-torial troops were brought up to keep it in repair and to double it by parallel tracks. Henceforward the tide of traffic reached the level of 6000 lorries in twenty-four hours. Pétain organized the front in sectors, each with its own heavy artillery, fixed a line which had to be held at all costs, and threw in repeated counterattacks. If these gained little ground, they disconcerted and checked the attacking Germans. The advance lost its momentum, slowed down, and although the Germans tried to widen the front of attack to the west bank of the Meuse, they were too late, and by March 8 the immediate danger of a break-through was past. But the very publicity given to the defense had endowed Verdun with a symbolical value definitely superior to its military value.

The Germans adopted an attrition policy which was helped by their closeness to the town, and although their advances were slight, they were cumulative in effect, like the erosion of the tide. Worse still, owing to the Germans' clever tactics, the balance of loss now turned against the defender. It was the irony of fate that Pétain, so instinctively saving in lives, should have had to violate his principles in order to be the savior of Verdun. He did his best to mitigate the strain on the men by a rapid *roulement* of reliefs, which kept each division under fire for the shortest possible time. But as a result, nearly all the French army was drawn through the mill, and the *usure* of force crippled the French effort in the projected Somme offensive, throwing the main burden on the British. If this offensive, which began on July 1, was disappointing in its direct results, it at once brought relief to Verdun. From that day on, the Germans at Verdun received no new divisions and their advance died out from sheer inanition.

Pétain rightly earned great prestige from this long-sustained defense, but it is just to recognize that his influence there was rather as an organizer than as a commander. On May 1 he had been promoted to command of the Centre Army Group, and Nivelle succeeded him in charge of the Second Army, which was actually defending Verdun.

After July, the distraction caused by the Somme offensive enabled plans to be made for regaining lost ground, and on October 21 and November 15 Mangin conducted those brilliant counteroffensives, highly economical because of their meticulous organization, which retook by bites what had been lost by nibbles.

It was yet another jest of fortune that the personal fruits of these successes should be reaped neither by the man who had devised the method nor by the man who had executed it. For when, in December 1916, the rising tide of dissatisfaction compelled the deposition of Joffre as Commander in Chief, Nivelle was called to fill his place. Public opinion contrasted the costly nibbles of the Somme strategy with the dazzling but economical autumn offensives at Verdun, which they associated primarily with Nivelle. This public opinion, however, was not entirely a natural growth.

Pétain was passed over partly because he had raised hostility, and partly because his strength of purpose affrighted the ruling clique, political and

military. When Poincaré and Pétain, both shy men
under a brusque cloak, had met at Verdun, they had
jarred on each other, and an inapt question had
drawn from Pétain the blunt reply that France could
not hope to win with her existing Government. If
the President of the Republic was later to understand
and appreciate Pétain, this burst of candor helped
to lose him the command in chief. But there was
another cause. Joffre's staff tended to lay the blame
for the popular discontent on the man whose constant
demands for troops at Verdun had denuded them of
reserves and thus, in their opinion, contributed to
the failure on the Somme. Feeling that Joffre was
doomed, they set themselves to pave the way for the
succession of Nivelle, through whom they felt more
confident of preserving their own control than if
Pétain came.

The new régime, however, was short-lived, for the
failure of Nivelle's grandiose offensive in April
wrought his downfall. His trouble was that, while
he focused the end correctly, he took too little account
of the means. When by the astute German retreat
to the Hindenburg Line the bases of his scheme were
uprooted, he still clung to it, and, surprised himself,
gave away all attempt at surprising the enemy in a
scheme which could succeed only by surprise. Only
one of Pétain's armies was concerned in this offensive.
At the preliminary council of war his opinion had
been against the unlimited objectives prescribed,

and immediately after the initial check he urged that the offensive should be broken off. The Government, disillusioned by the heavy losses and slight gains, lacked the courage either to stop Nivelle or to back him, and their petty interference merely sapped the confidence of all ranks. Ultimately, on April 28, they appointed Pétain Chief of the French General Staff, as a brake on the offensive and as a step from which he could mount into Nivelle's seat. By May 15 the Ministers plucked up sufficient courage to depose Nivelle, and Pétain reigned in his place. This time it was a moral Verdun which he was called upon to save. Indeed, he was the type of man whose services a democracy would only call on in a dark hour. So long as the sun shines, and even when shadows draw in, the people like men who will pander to their illusions and promise them more sunny hours.

Pétain's first mission was to restore the French army, its strength and its morale. Mutinies had broken out, and if actual anarchy was the exception, refusal to obey orders was widespread. To some extent it was due to defeatist and Communist propaganda, but in far greater measure to service grievances and war weariness. The leaders might still be full of the *offensive à outrance*, or the doctrine of attrition, but the troops were sick of being thrown against barbed wire and machine guns to no apparent effect, and they could see no difference between Joffre's nibbling and Nivelle's "break-through" strategy, except that in one the losses were spread out and in the other concentrated. Sixteen army corps were affected, and the trouble generally arose with troops ordered back to the trenches from rest.

Faced with a crumbling army, Pétain adopted the same policy that Scipio, another supreme psychologist, had practised at Sucro two thousand years before — a fearless and firm call to duty, combined with prompt remedy of just grievances. Had he read his Polybius? For a month his car traveled up and down the front, visiting nearly every division. He summoned not merely officers, but men from the ranks, before him, and asked them frankly for their complaints, while strongly rebuking the crime of mutiny in face of the enemy. Essentially patriarchal and not familiar, he inspired confidence in his firm control as well as in his promises. Tours of duty in the trenches were made equal, regularity of leave ensured, rest camps improved. Within a month tranquillity was restored, with hardly a dozen executions. But if the army was convalescent, he had still to revive its fighting confidence and power. To this end he reorganized the training, prescribed the new method of defense in depth, and recast the offensive tactics in such a manner that fire-power should so far as possible replace men in the attack. Finally, he tempered his weapon afresh by a few strictly limited attacks, which by cheaply won success should consolidate the reborn confidence of the troops. Such were

Guillaumat's attack at Verdun in August, which regained the whole of the ground lost in 1916, and Maistre's attack at Malmaison in October, which captured the whole of the famous Chemin des Dames ridge.

"Going slow" was the only possible policy, but it meant that the French army was practically out of action for the remainder of 1917, and meanwhile the British had to bear the whole burden. Perhaps they shouldered it too generously and unwisely, thus leaving themselves so weakened that they were a ready prey to the dangers of 1918.

But if Pétain, in his concern for the restoration of the French army, left much to his allies, it is just to record that when the British achieved their great tank surprise at Cambrai in November, Pétain had assembled strong French reënforcements in the Senlis-Peronne area and set them in motion directly the attack was launched. It remains one of the mysteries of the war why their support was not called upon, the more so that the splendid opportunity offered by this new tank method was lost through lack of British reserves.

On the heels of this battle followed the bitter controversy over the Versailles Council and the question of the unity of command. Pétain, unlike most of the French and British commanders, was not a Western Front fanatic, and had been an advocate of wider operations against the strategic flank of the

Germanic Alliance — he was too much of a realist
to shut his eyes to the futility of attrition or a break-
through until a new key was found. Hence his opposition to the Supreme War Council did not spring
from a hidebound Westernism. But, like his opposite number, Haig, he distrusted committee control,
and preferred to make a direct arrangement with
Haig for mutual support in face of the looming menace of a German offensive. Nevertheless, he was to
be the indirect cause of the breakdown of this arrangement.

Pétain was thoroughly convinced of the danger
and stood firm against all pressure and clamor to
harry him into either a premature or a preventive
offensive. In the light of after-knowledge we can
realize that such a move would not only have
been ineffectual but have bankrupted the Allied
cause, for their margin of reserves barely held out in
the pure defensive the next spring. As a further safeguard, he wished to adopt the system of elastic
defense which was to be so effective in July 1918,
but the Government attached an exaggerated moral
value to the ground, and thus condemned themselves
to lose by miles what they might only have relinquished by yards — *pour mieux sauter*. Pétain was
immovable before political pressure where it impinged
on his dominant sense of caution, but he yielded to
its influence on matters that seemed to him less
menacing to the security of France. Herein lay the

cause of the breakdown of the scheme for coöperation between the Allied armies.

The initial source was that while the British Intelligence, rightly, predicted the German offensive on the St. Quentin front, the French, wrongly, anticipated it in Champagne. When the blow fell on March 21, they believed that it was only a feint preceding the real blow on their own front, and in consequence the promised support was somewhat slow to arrive, although its numerical strength was certainly in excess of the limited pledge originally given. Moreover, when the German flood surged forward so rapidly that it seemed Amiens must fall, he informed Haig on March 24 that the reserves then concentrating near Montdidier would have to be withdrawn southwestward in order to cover the approach to Paris. This would have meant the separation of the Allied armies. It was averted by the Doullens Conference and the appointment of Foch to coördinate the action of the whole front — a measure whose immediate purpose was to prevent this cleavage.

But if Pétain failed to take long views in this crisis, he was large-hearted enough to respond loyally to the orders of Foch, the man whom a year before he had rescued from semiretirement. And if thenceforth he played a subordinate rôle in the strategy of the campaign, he was fertile in tactical expedients, showing all his old quickness to recognize the possibilities of new weapons. Thus on the evening of March 23, while at dinner, he interrupted the meal to issue a sudden order for the available air squadrons to be dispatched for a surprise counterattack, like cavalry of the air, on the German divisions coming up to carry on the advance.

Pétain's own turn to bear the brunt of battle came in May, when the German torrent broke by surprise through the Aisne front and swept to the banks of the Marne in four days. The surprise was primarily due to the defects of the French Intelligence Service and to the blindness and overbearing obstinacy of General Duchêne, the Sixth Army commander, who refused to listen to the warnings both from his own subordinates and the commanders of the British divisions which had been sent to this "quiet sector" to rest. Pétain must bear some of the responsibility for retaining a commander who had long been a source of friction and distrust, but he acted promptly and wisely in stemming the westward expansion of the flood. And he divined and was ready for the German attempt, which followed on June 9, to break down the buttress left between the bulges they had made in March and May respectively. To meet this attack he experimented with his plan of elastic defense — yielding the first position to the enemy, and then, when their advance had lost its momentum and order, offering a thoroughly prepared resistance on the second position. Owing to the innate con-

servatism of the commanders on the spot, obsessed
with the tradition of holding on to every yard of
ground, the experiment was only a partial success —
for which the local command was castigated by
Pétain. But it paved the way for July 15, when the
final German onslaught, east of Rheims, was completely dislocated by this method, surprising the
would-be surprisers. As at Verdun, so at Rheims.
By the irony of fortune popular opinion called this
"Gouraud's manœuvre," although Pétain had taken
a week to persuade this lion-hearted leader to fall in
with his plan of yielding up the forward position.
If Pétain countermanded the historic counterstroke,
which Foch ordered to continue, it is unjust to
suggest that he intended more than a temporary
postponement, for whereas Foch had wished to anticipate the enemy's offensive by his own, Pétain's
conception had been that of the defensive-offensive
battle as it was actually waged — first to parry the
enemy's thrust and then a riposte when he was off his
balance.

He had gauged the situation aright after checking the previous German attack, when, forsaking his
habitual caution, he had prophesied : "If we can
hold on until the end of June, our situation will be
excellent. In July we can resume the offensive;
after that, victory will be ours." With more insight
into material factors than Foch, — whose mind had
been filled with dreams of this offensive while the

German blows were still falling, — Pétain had realized that the scales turned on the flow of American reën-forcements, and that the essential factor was to keep his forces unbroken until the Americans tilted the balance against Germany. July 18 and its sequel were the vindication of his judgment and atoned for any momentary short sight in March.

In the actual advance to victory, skillful as was his combination of penetrative advances with suc-cessive lateral exploitations, Pétain played a lesser rôle, partly because the strategical direction was in the hands of Foch, and partly because the de-cisive work was done by the British and American forces. If this was natural, because they formed the two horns of the advancing masses, it must be admitted that the French in the centre fell in admirably with this manœuvre, threatening the enemy by their presence but not hurrying his retreat from the bag which the British and Americans were steadily closing. The French advance usually kept a step in the rear, moving forward when their allies on the flanks had pushed back the enemy. Thus Pétain's life-saving policy not merely preserved the French army until the tide turned, but preserved it until peace was won. On November 21, 1918, after the triumphal entry into the redeemed city of Metz, Pétain received the Marshal's baton that he had so well earned of his country. He had proved himself one of the first, and one of the few, leaders to understand the mechanism of modern war as it had been developed by industrial nations in arms. In such warfare the artist was at a loss, but Pétain had contributed the keen perception and supreme organizing power that were essential.

Moreover, he was a profound psychologist. Where Foch knew only his own soul, Pétain penetrated into the thoughts and feelings of the men in the trenches, the people in arms. And to the sordid business which warfare had become he imparted a current of personal magnetism, otherwise rare among the higher command. His justness, his sympathy, his thoroughness, were all sources of his hold on men's affections, but there was more. For example, it was a custom of his to visit a regiment, have a dozen men called out of the ranks, and ask them to name the bravest man in the regiment. When they had come to a decision, Pétain there and then would pin the Legion of Honor on the breast of the officer or man they had chosen.

As a commander he has been reproached for excessive caution. It would be more true to say that he was excessively careful — of lives. While the motto of a brilliant fighting leader like Mangin was "victory at any price," Pétain's motto was "victory at the smallest price." This instinct sprang less from caution than from realism. Like a ray of light, his vision pierced the conventional mist of pre-war military ideas, in search of truth. He even carried his love of truth so far that, unlike his predecessors, he set his face against ambiguous reports which covered up ill success and against any propaganda by his staff. Self-discipline and self-effacement replaced flattery and intrigue.

For want of opportunity, history may not rate him among the great strategists. And it would seem that he was more an inventor of tactical methods than an executive tactician. But it is almost certain that the French army would never have recovered if Pétain had not been called to command in 1917. He made victory possible. If Foch, for all his great qualities, or any other offensive-inspired general had been appointed instead, the war would have been lost, for France at least.

Thus the verdict of history on Pétain is likely to read: "The man who, like Fabius, saved his country by avoiding battle, and who, like Carnot, was the organizer of victory."

ALLENBY OF MEGIDDO

THE EVOLUTION OF A LEADER

ALLENBY OF MEGIDDO

THE EVOLUTION OF A LEADER

FEW famous men have been the object of such extremes of condemnation and admiration within the space of a few years as Allenby. It may be replied that these extremes are not so uncommon, that the crowd is always fickle in its favors. But the verdict came not from popular opinion, which knew him not until he was famous; it came from his peers and his subordinates, who were in close touch with him during the four years of the World War. Most curious of all was the sharp dividing line drawn by a journey through the Mediterranean in June 1917. For almost three years in France he had been the target of strong criticism, lessening only in degree in the later part of this time — criticism not lightly to be discounted, because it came from many quarters and from men whose honesty and judgment were, and still are, held in the highest respect. Then he left to take over the command of the Egyptian Expeditionary Force, and from that moment on his reputation became as radiantly white as formerly it had been black. Nor was the change due to military success. Men may win victories which crown them with popular glory, but victory does not blind their co-workers to the existence of their defects. It is proverbial that no man is a hero to his valet, and few generals are immaculate in the eyes of their staff and subordinate commanders, however loyal these may be in comment at the time, or however much they may admire their chief on balance. Yet Allenby in Palestine became, as a chief, not only preponderant in his good qualities, but "sans reproche" for any bad qualities. By no means a human enigma, his career is an historical enigma. By no means a romantic type, he conducted one of history's most romantic campaigns, in its site, sequence, method, and result — the last Crusade.

An East Midlander by birth and having an ancestral link with Oliver Cromwell, Edmund Henry Hynman Allenby was born at Southwell in Nottinghamshire on April 23, 1861. Educated at an East Anglian school, Haileybury, he was intended for the Indian Civil Service, but failed in this stiff examination and, following his own inclinations, entered the army instead. From the Royal Military College, Sandhurst, he passed to a commission in the Inniskilling Dragoons, whom he joined in South Africa during 1882. It has fallen to few young officers to go on active service so early in their career and to share in so many, if minor, expeditions. A year after joining he was in the Zululand campaign which ended in King Cetewayo's surrender; in 1885 he served with the Bechuanaland expedition; and in 1888, promoted captain after less than six years' service, he was back again in Zululand to take part in the crushing of Dinizulu's rebellion. Thereafter he passed into the Staff College, where he was more celebrated for his appetite and hard riding than for professional distinction. But his popularity with his fellows led him to be elected master of the drag — over Haig's head, incidentally. After leaving Camberley, his career took a slower course until the Boer War came to his relief. He then gave up a staff appointment to go out again, in command of a squadron, to the land where he had first seen service.

Early in 1900, in charge of a small mixed column, he made a wide outflanking move against the enemy's communications, which brought him to notice and was a foretaste of that bold sense and conception of manœuvre which later distinguished him. He was in command of his own regiment during the advance to Pretoria, and of a column in the "sweeping" operations against the Boer guerrilla bands later, and at the end of the war was promoted lieutenant colonel and given command of the 5th (Royal Irish) Lancers. Yet in comparison with another great leader of the World War, born in the same year, Haig, he had lost ground, despite having been a more successful column leader. For although Haig had been commissioned three years later than Allenby, he was a full colonel at the end of the South African

War and a major general less than two years after.
The difference created by that campaign was to have
a vital influence on the fortunes of the two cavalry-
men and on the destiny of the command in France
thirteen years later. Yet, if Allenby was to forfeit
the greater prize, it may well have been to the
advantage of his place in history. And even that
lost prize was nearly restored to him by a turn of
Fortune's wheel, for it is within the knowledge of
those who followed the devious undercurrents of war
politics in 1914–1918 that several times an eddy
nearly swept him into the place of the man who had
overtaken and passed him in South Africa.

Not until 1909, five years after Haig, did Allenby
reach major general's rank, although at forty-eight
he was by ordinary standards youthful for this
rank. Next year he became Inspector of Cavalry
and the commander designate of the cavalry of the
Expeditionary Force.

In training the cavalry of the Home Army, "the
Bull," as Allenby was universally called, proved
himself as determined and uncompromising in pursuit of his ideal of efficiency as he had been when in
command of a regiment. To the slack or incom-
petent he gave short shrift, but his discrimination
was not always so good as his intention. And his
impatience with diverging views and in sweeping
aside reasonable explanations not infrequently
created, among the best subordinates, a sense of

injustice or aggravation, which was enhanced and gained point from the fact that his handling of the cavalry on manœuvres was by no means faultless.

On the outbreak of war in August 1914, Allenby went out to France as commander of the Cavalry Division, which originally consisted of four instead of three brigades. Prior to the opening clash at Mons on August 22 the Cavalry Division had only succeeded in giving the British Command the vaguest warning of the hostile masses which were closing upon and threatening to surround the little British Expeditionary Force. This failure to fulfill its true rôle was due, however, primarily to the dispositions of the British Commander in Chief, who placed the cavalry at the outset on his right rear, which was also the flank of least danger. Indeed, these dispositions were not only a direct but an indirect source of harm. For when Sir John French, on his way to the front, called on his neighbor Lanrezac, commanding the French Fifth Army on his eastern flank, and explained his dispositions, Lanrezac formed such a low opinion of a man who could thus place his cavalry behind his infantry, when information and security were all important, that he lost all faith in his British neighbor. Hence arose the friction and disunity of action between the neighboring armies which persisted throughout the retreat.

When the British moved forward on August 21, — pushing their heads, in ignorance, into the German noose, — the Cavalry Division was moved over to the left flank. And when that tentative advance changed into defense at Mons, on August 23, Allenby's troops prolonged the British left, covering the exposed western flank.

In the early hours of August 24 Sir John French issued orders for a retreat, to draw back if possible out of the noose, with the Cavalry Division covering the retirement of Smith-Dorrien's 2nd Army Corps. When the 2nd Corps halted at Le Cateau next evening, Allenby visited Smith-Dorrien and told him that the Cavalry Division was too scattered and the horses too tired for him to continue covering the retirement next day, and that the infantry must get away during the night if they were to avoid capture by the Germans, close on their heels. Allenby only gave this warning at 2 A.M., and it was impossible at such short notice for the infantry, footsore and partly distributed in defensive positions, to get on the move again before daylight. Thus Smith-Dorrien's men were forced to stand and fight unsupported, escaping disaster only by their splendid resistance and at a heavy price. In the morning the cavalry continued their retirement, except the 1st (Briggs) and 3rd (Gough) Cavalry Brigades, which stayed behind independently to cover the right rear of the 2nd Corps. When Smith-Dorrien's men fell back that evening, exhausted and disordered, it was fortunate that the German pursuit was tardy and then took the wrong direction; but it was also fortunate that Smith-Dorrien's left, the more exposed flank, was protected by Sordet's French Cavalry Corps, for there were no British cavalry on this vital flank.

It is necessary for the historian, however unwillingly, to correct a popular delusion which gained color both from the Commander in Chief's dispatches and his later comment, that "the cavalry, under Allenby's skillful direction, was effectively holding off the enemy's pursuit."

In blunt fact, Allenby, during the most critical phase, did not direct the cavalry operations in covering the retreat, because a large part of his division had escaped from his control. And as there was known friction between him and some of his subordinates, this escape was perhaps not involuntary — such, at least, is the belief of other eminent soldiers. Whether this be so or not, it is at least certain that at one time Allenby's Division, for practical purposes, consisted of little more than himself and his staff. Not until August 30 were three of the four brigades reunited under his control, and the other — the 3rd — never rejoined, remaining away on the right. On the eve of the Battle of the Marne its commander, Gough, took the 5th Cavalry Brigade under his wing, and on September 16 these two brigades were officially designated the 2nd Cavalry Division.

When the British faced about on September 6, after retreating a day's march farther south than their neighbors, the Cavalry Division under Allenby was kept on the right rear of the infantry during the first two days of the advance, covering the flank, although the vital need was for the British to retrace their steps at full speed and pierce the weak joint of the enemy line opposite them. Only on September 11, when the Germans had been in retreat for two days, was the Cavalry Division tentatively unleashed in pursuit by Sir John French, giving the Germans time to recover and, on September 14, block the British advance across the Aisne — a resistance which ushered in four years of trench warfare. When the British Expeditionary Force was transferred from the Aisne to Flanders, in the vain attempt of the Allies to find and turn the Germans' open flank, the infantry went by rail, but the cavalry by march route through Picardy. During that move, on October 9, the two cavalry divisions were fused into a Cavalry Corps, under Allenby.

Directly on arrival, the British advance began, by the 2nd Corps, while the Cavalry Corps moved forward along an arc to the north, covering the detrainment of the 3rd Corps and then advancing on its left, French having the idea that the "plains of Flanders" were excellent ground for cavalry shock action! If the advance was short-lived, the Cavalry Corps secured the valuable Messines-Wytschaete ridges before the advance changed to a desperate dismounted defense. Moreover, if they were stretched

out perilously thin, they had linked up on the left
with the hard-pressed defenders of Ypres, and thus
a complete if slender barrier was opposed to the
German masses who were incessantly hurled against
it during the following weeks in the effort to break
through to the Channel ports. Although forced to
yield the Messines ridge, the dismounted cavalry,
stiffened by infantry reënforcements, maintained
their front unbroken until at last French relief came.
In this "soldiers' battle" Allenby, like other generals,
could do no more than strive to mend the crumbling
parts of his front, but in this process, cemented by
ultimate success, he bore a responsibility only less
than that of Haig.

In the trench warfare which followed there was no
scope for cavalry, and many cavalry soldiers began
to change to the command of infantry formations,
among them Allenby. Appropriately, it was during
the crisis of the second battle of Ypres — the first gas
attack — that Allenby was summoned to take charge
of the threatened 5th Corps in the Ypres salient. If
the immediate danger was averted, the drain of lives
was heavy throughout the summer, perhaps heavier
than necessary, and it is at least certain that the 5th
Corps command acquired a reputation of ill-omen
among the troops. So much so that when a certain
division, perhaps the best in France in 1915, received
word that it was to be transferred to Allenby's
Corps, the depression and morale decline were so

marked that the consequences were pointed out to
G. H. Q. and it was sent instead to another corps in
the same area.

One source of complaint at Ypres was that the
offensive spirit of the commander was not balanced
by adequate investigation and knowledge of the
situation. For example, a counterattack was ordered
to recapture a supposed strong point which was found
to have no existence except on a paper plan, and
only the moral courage of the local commander in
disobeying orders averted a heavy and pointless
waste of life — but nearly brought his own dismissal.
The swelling strength of the British forces had
already led to their being divided into two armies,
and in the late summer of 1915 a Third Army was
formed when the British took over the French
sector between the Ancre and the Somme. Monro,
who at "First Ypres" had been a divisional commander in Haig's Corps when Allenby was the
Cavalry Corps commander, was given command,
but in October he was sent to take charge of the
Dardenelles force, and Allenby stepped into his
place — the last big appointment that Sir John
French made before he was replaced as Commander
in Chief by Haig.

Allenby was thus in charge of the sector where the
main British offensive of 1916 was planned to take
place, but some months before it was launched Allenby's army was side-stepped to the north, between

the Ancre and Arras, and a new Fourth Army under Rawlinson was inserted to conduct the main offensive on the Somme. Thus the Third Army's share on July 1 was limited to a subsidiary attack with two divisions, against the Gommecourt salient, which met with an almost more bloody repulse than the main attack to the south. During the rest of the year Allenby had to remain inactive while the battles of the Somme were raging on his flank, a share of the offensive being now taken over by a new Fifth Army, under Gough, which had been pushed in between Rawlinson and Allenby.

But in the spring of 1917 an attacking rôle was at last assigned to Allenby, and when the time came almost the whole burden of the offensive fell to him. For the Germans' strategic retreat to the Hindenburg Line dislocated the intended renewal of the offensive on the Somme by the artificial desert which it had created for the armies of Gough and Rawlinson to cross. The German retreat had flattened out their former pinch-inviting salient, and from Arras south-eastward ran the tremendous defenses of the new Hindenburg Line. If Allenby could break through the old defenses just to the north of where this line ended, he would automatically take it in flank and rear, but in anticipation of such a move the Germans had dug a switch line from Quéant, near the northern end of the Hindenburg Line, through Drocourt, covering the rear of their old defenses north of Arras.

Thus Allenby's whole chance of strategic success depended on whether he could reach and break through this partially completed switch line — some five miles behind the front system — before the German reserves could arrive in strength. Surprise was the only key which could open this gate. Because of this the real drama of the Arras offensive lies in the preliminary discussions more than in the battle itself. Surprise had been almost discarded in the Somme offensive; indeed, this master key of all the Great Captains of history had been left to rust since the spring of 1915. Would it be brought out afresh in order to open the way to the Drocourt-Quéant switch within the brief time before the door was bolted and barred by the German reserves?

The two means by which surprise and time could be gained were by launching a mass of tanks as at Cambrai in the autumn, or by a hurricane bombardment with gas, brief but intense. The first means was impossible, owing to the slowness in delivering new tanks after the discouraging reports made upon them in 1916, so that sixty old machines were all that could be scraped together. Allenby and his artillery adviser were anxious to have the shortest possible artillery bombardment, and proposed that it should last only twenty-four hours. If this, according to later standards, was twenty hours too long, it was a tentative step in the direction of surprise. But General Headquarters were too material-minded to appreciate it, and had a deep-rooted distrust of such an innovation. Against their remonstrances, however, Allenby stood firm, until they hit on the device of promoting his artillery adviser to another sphere and replacing him by one imbued with their own views.

Allenby then gave way, and the plan of a five days' bombardment, preceded by three weeks of systematic wire-cutting, was adopted — to the doom of surprise and the abnegation of a break-through. Allenby's yielding on this point against his own convictions seems hardly in keeping with his reputation for strength of character, although it may be urged that, as a cavalryman, it was not easy for him to overrule the advice of an artillery expert. But where experts differ a general is justified in basing his choice on his own common sense, in the light of the fundamental principles of war.

In smaller points he still sought for surprise, notably in opening up the underground quarries of Arras, St. Sauveur, and Ronville in order to shelter two divisions which were to pass underground and leap-frog through the leading divisions. Another feature of the plan was that, after the three assaulting corps of the Third Army had broken the enemy's first system of defense, the Cavalry Corps and the 18th Corps were to pass through in the centre between the human buttresses and drive forward toward the switch line. Partly for concealment, the daring risk was taken of moving this pursuit force through the city of Arras, whose houses extended almost up to the front line. This plan, refreshingly ingenious, was vitiated, however, by two factors. First, the absence of initial surprise; second, the comparatively narrow front of the opening attack, — little more than ten miles, — so that the central bottle-neck was, in turn, so narrow that its end could be easily stopped. Ludendorff in his Vilna offensive in the autumn of 1915 had revealed a better method — a dual penetration by two horns goring their way into the enemy front, while through the wide gap between the horns the pursuit force unexpectedly issued.

A fundamental defect of the Arras plan, moreover, was that its base was far wider than its fighting front — the routes of supply and reënforcement all converging on Arras, with the result that the narrow mouth of this bottle-neck became utterly congested. When the initial attack failed to make the progress anticipated, this congestion was increased by the arrival of the cavalry in the forward area, although it should have been clear from the experience of the Somme that this advance was futile unless and until a wide path had been swept clear of the enemy. The results of the opening attack were greater and quicker, both in prisoners and progress, than any previous offensive, yet they extinguished the possibility of a strategic break-through, for only a miracle could have recovered the chance that had been dissipated almost completely before the attack was launched.

In the attempt to redeem the fading strategic hopes, Allenby's resolution was more marked than his understanding of modern fire-power. To assist his frontal advance eastward he insisted that the divisions facing the Hindenburg Line should make a convergent attack from the southwest, disregarding the fact — and the protests — that they had insufficient artillery to subdue these formidable defenses. From this project, which must have cost a fruitless sacrifice of lives, he was luckily dissuaded — circumstantial evidence suggests that it was by the personal intervention of Haig, who was visiting this sector. And when the distant French offensive on the Aisne, to which the Arras battle was the preliminary, proved abortive, Allenby's renewed series of blunt attacks, some in conjunction with the Fifth Army, were merely an object lesson in the most expensive way of trying to occupy the enemy's attention. They were closed down on May 5, and next month Allenby was sent from France to replace Sir Archibald Murray, French's old chief of staff during the retreat from Mons, in command of the Egyptian Expeditionary Force, which had twice failed disastrously to break the Turkish defenses at Gaza.

That sea voyage was a turning point in Allenby's

career as well as in his reputation, both as commander and man. The clouding obsessions of the
later phase at Arras were blown away, leaving the
impressions of hard experience to broaden and refine
the original instinct for surprise. It is a moot point
whether, if he had stayed in France, he would ever
have adapted himself to the conditions of siege warfare as well as Haig ultimately did. And a recall to
France, to take the supreme command, was later a
possibility. But it is doubtful whether any other
leader if sent to Palestine would have been Allenby's
equal in boldness of conception and extent of success.
For in this theatre of war, where the historic methods
of attack were still feasible when directed with
vigor, inspired by surprise, and attuned to modern
weapons, Allenby found the right field for his gifts
and instincts.

In France siege warfare was too firmly consolidated
to be dissolved by merely ringing the changes upon
traditional methods; in Palestine an alternative to
siege warfare was possible, and it could be exploited
if surprise was brought to bear.

Gaza, on the coast, and Beersheba, thirty-five
miles inland, form the two natural gateways into
Palestine, and between them lie a series of ridges
which form a natural wall easily capable of defense.
The British force, after dragging its weary length
across the Sinai Desert from Egypt, had tried in vain
to force the strongly fortified Gaza gate. Beersheba,

less artificially strong, was protected by the difficulty of transport and water supply for an attacking force.

Experience had shown Allenby that even the most difficult manœuvre was preferable to butting directly against a blank wall. Grown receptive, he had no hesitation, after study of the position, in adopting the plan outlined in an appreciation made by Chetwode, the commander on the spot, while improving its details by the light of his own experience. With a heightened understanding of the axiom that the success of an attack is in proportion to the firm security of the base from which it is launched, he devoted himself to intensive preparation — of communications, water supply, training — during his first three months on the borders of Palestine, while the season was still unsuitable for operations. Not less significant was that he moved General Headquarters up from Cairo to the front, at Rafa, where he could have his finger on the pulse of battle, and of his troops. It was not only a sound military move but a wise human move, acting both as an ointment to sore feelings — for men could not help contrasting their hardships in the desert with the supposed enjoyment of Cairo amenities by the arbiters of their fate — and as a tonic, because the presence of their chief was to the men a visible guaranty that they would not be thrown into the attack without due study and knowledge of the situation. Even to the natives of the country Allenby's coming carried a mystic significance, for the Arabic form of his name, "Allah Nebi," meant "the Prophet of God," and thus appeared the complement, in the eyes of a superstitious people, to the old prophecy that when the waters of the Nile flowed into Palestine the land would be freed from the domination of the Turk — a condition that had been fulfilled by the construction of a pipe line across the desert.

Furthermore, Allenby's determination enabled him to insist on and obtain the force necessary for his plan, a reënforcement which his precedessor had not obtained. Thus Allenby obtained a full two-to-one superiority over his enemy — not excessive if he was to gain decisive results and in view of the increased resisting power of a defender under modern conditions. The enemy, on their side, were also planning an offensive to drive the British back into the desert, but Allenby struck first. By thorough precautions for secrecy and many ruses he misled the Turks as to the real point of attack. The defenses of Gaza were bombarded from October 26 onward, and as a deception to Turkish eyes the camps behind the British lines were left standing with rows of empty tents, whose occupants were on the move toward Beersheba. At dawn on October 31 two British infantry divisions attacked its defenses from the southwest while two mounted divisions, Anzac and Australian, were closing on the town from the east, and in the afternoon a daring cavalry

charge over the narrow trenches captured this
gateway to Palestine and its essential water-supply.
Next, to maintain the delusion that this attack was
only a diversion, a strong holding attack was made
on the Gaza defenses during the night of November 1. The new enemy commander, Falkenhayn, also aided Allenby's plan by throwing in his
reserves in a vain counterattack to regain Beersheba
and thus had no reserves left when, at dawn on
November 6, Allenby's main and decisive blow fell
on the Turkish left centre, and broke through into
the Plain of Philistia. The mounted pursuit, hampered by lack of water, was also less able in execution
than the battle had been in conception, and by a
prompt retreat from Gaza the Turks avoided being
cut off. Nevertheless, by November 14, the port of
Jaffa had been seized, giving Allenby sea communication with Egypt; the Turkish force driven apart
into two divergent masses; and, leaving a detach-
ment to watch the mass which had retreated up the
coast, Allenby wheeled east for an advance inland
against Jerusalem.

It was difficult to supply his whole force, and so
Allenby took the sound risk of pushing on at full
speed with a part to secure the mountain passes
before the Turks could block them. He succeeded,
and although a stout Turkish resistance, almost at
the gates of Jerusalem, brought his rush to a halt, he
had passed the worst obstacles, so that the arrival of

reënforcements enabled him to capture the Turkish trenches and open the way to the Holy City, which was surrendered on December 9. Two days later Allenby entered the city on foot by the historic Jaffa gate, specially reopened for the purpose, thus offering a contrast with the theatrical mounted entry of the Kaiser in 1898, for whose convenience and glorification a breach had been made in the city wall. Allenby's next step was to secure his hold on Jerusalem and Jaffa by securing sufficient room for manœuvre in front of these cities, and the repulse of Falkenhayn's misguided attempt to retake Jerusalem enabled the British, on the rebound, to gain ample space to safeguard their possession of Jerusalem.

Allenby's advance was resumed in February 1918, and his first step was to make his eastern flank secure as a preliminary to a northward move. Jericho and the river line of the Jordan had been gained when the crisis in France caused by the German offensive — Ludendorff's last throw for victory — forced Allenby to dispatch thither most of his British troops. The depletion was made up by troops from India, and Allenby, undaunted, devoted the summer to the reorganization and training of these Indian units, building up a fresh striking force for the decisive stroke he had in mind. To pave the way, Allenby launched two raids east of the Jordan, in March and May, in order to create the impression that he intended to advance up the Hejaz railway, which ran parallel with

ALLENBY ENTERING JERUSALEM

and about thirty miles east of the Jordan, linking
Arabia with Damascus. Allenby had already decided to make his real blow on the western flank in
the coastal plain, where he could exploit his superiority in mounted troops, and his aim was therefore to
draw the Turkish reserves over to the opposite flank.
If neither of the raids was a full success tactically, they
fulfilled their strategic object, for the threat led the
new enemy commander, Liman von Sanders, to place
one third of his total force henceforth on the east of
the Jordan.

In this farsighted strategy of "mystify, mislead,
and surprise," Allenby had a new and important
ally. Far away to the south, in Arabia, the Hejaz
had risen in revolt against the Turk in 1916, under
Hussein, the Sherif of Mecca. This pin-prick was
converted into a dagger-thrust through the appearance of a young Englishman, Lawrence, with an
acute understanding of Arab psychology and a genius
for guerrilla warfare, based on an inversion of the
orthodox rules of strategy. He persuaded Feisal,
son of Hussein and commander of the Arab forces,
to neglect the Turkish armed forces in Arabia and
to spread the revolt, like lighting a prairie fire, in
their rear northward to Damascus, combining propaganda with continual raids on the long-drawn-out
line of the Hejaz railway. To Lawrence's strategic
ideas and his appeals for equipment and camels
Allenby was sympathetic, one more proof of his new

receptiveness, and his support was an aid to Lawrence in dealing with more conventional and shortersighted members of his staff.

The outcome was that in September 1918 Lawrence and the Arab army were both a psychological and a material aid to Allenby's plan. By circling round the rear of the Turkish army east of the Jordan, they cut the Damascus railway round the vital junction of Deraa, where the lines to the Hejaz and to Palestine diverged. Thus they not only attracted Turkish attention away from Allenby's real point of attack, but closed the only railway line of retreat and supply to all the Turkish armies.

Allenby also turned to profit another new weapon — aircraft. On September 17 and 18 bombing raids cut the telegraph and telephone wires leading from the Turkish General Headquarters at Nazareth back along their line of communications, and on the night before the attack, September 18–19, a further raid on Afule destroyed the wires leading from General Headquarters to the front. Thus the directing power of the enemy's brain was paralyzed.

Meanwhile the carefully shrouded preparations for the attack had been completed. Feinting toward the east bank of the Jordan to distract the enemy's attention afresh, the effect helped by a dummy concentration of troops in that area, Allenby secretly concentrated on the Mediterranean flank the mass of his infantry and behind them the cavalry,

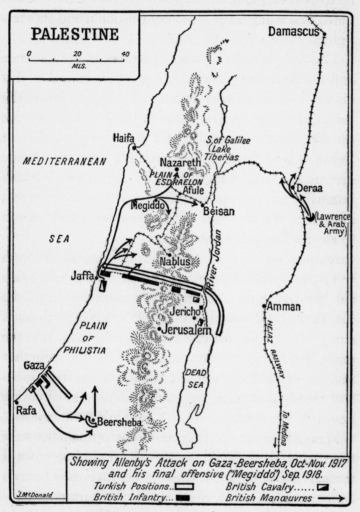

PALESTINE

0   20   40
MLS.

Damascus

Haifa

S. of Galilee
(Lake
Tiberias)

Nazareth

PLAIN OF
ESDRAELON

Afule

Deraa

Megiddo

Beisan

(Lawrence
& Arab
Army)

MEDITERRANEAN

SEA

Nablus

River Jordan

Jaffa

Amman

PLAIN
OF
PHILISTIA

Jericho

Jerusalem

HEJAZ RAILWAY

Gaza

DEAD
SEA

Rafa

Beersheba

To Medina

J.McDonald

Showing Allenby's Attack on Gaza-Beersheba, Oct.-Nov. 1917
and his final offensive ("Megiddo") Sep. 1918.
Turkish Positions...☐   British Cavalry......◩
British Infantry...■■   British Manœuvres ——➤

PALESTINE — ALLENBY'S CAMPAIGN

concealed in the orange and olive groves. Dust columns had gone eastward by day while troop columns marched westward by night. Thus he changed a two-to-one superiority on the front as a whole into a four-to-one superiority on the fifteen-mile sector chosen for the decisive attack, leaving forces actually inferior to the Turks on the remaining forty-five miles of front. On the night of September 18–19 these forces attacked in the hilly centre to fix the enemy's attention. At dawn, after only fifteen minutes' bombardment, the western mass was launched, and after breaking through the Turkish defenses wheeled to the right. Thus they rolled the Turks back northeast into the hills, like a door on its hinges.

Through the open doorway the cavalry passed, riding straight up the coastal corridor for thirty miles before swinging east to cut the Turkish communications and close all exits of retreat. One division captured Nazareth, fifty-two miles distant, twenty-four hours later; another covered the seventy miles to Beisan in thirty-four hours, and thus blocked the best line of retreat across the Jordan to Damascus. Completely trapped, the main Turkish armies were rounded up, while Allenby's cavalry exploited the victory of Megiddo by a swift and sustained pursuit which, in conjunction with the Arabs, pulverized the Turkish Fourth Army east of the Jordan, and gained first Damascus and later Aleppo. On October 31 the capitulation of Turkey rang down the curtain on this brief and dazzling campaign in which the British had advanced 360 miles in less than six weeks.

Making all allowances for the British superiority in strength, — against which must be set off the difficult country and the defensive power of modern weapons, — this campaign must still rank as one of the masterpieces of military history, as classic in execution as in design. The clean-cut decisiveness of the result was the product of the clear-sighted selection of objectives and the nicely calculated distribution of force. The plan, like the execution, was distinguished by its fulfillment of and extreme emphasis upon the principles of mobility and surprise, both strategic and tactical, which have ever been the hall mark of the Great Captains. And it was Napoleonic not merely in its shrewdly directed thrusts at the enemy's communications, but in its development of the British communications to coincide with the strategic plan, thus securing the offensive base from which the operations sprang and were maintained. In this campaign Allenby had a lesser superiority of strength than in his first, and the difference of result is partly to be explained by the difference in the security of his communications.

Some who knew only the Allenby of Mons and its sequel, Ypres, and Arras have found difficulty in understanding the apparent transformation of 1918. Thus, on the one hand, there has been a tendency to discount this masterpiece unduly because of Allenby's superiority of strength. And, on the other, there has been a tendency, natural in view of the many other instances, to look for the brain of a staff officer behind the form of the commander — to ask who was Allenby's Weygand, if not his Ludendorff. The fact that in this last year he had in charge of the Operations Branch, Bartholomew, whose great ability was universally recognized, lent color to such speculations, which, as is usually the result, were rather fostered than dissipated by the extreme loyalty of Bartholomew, a second Weygand in his self-effacement. But, in fact, there are the strongest grounds for the verdict that, while the detailed working out of the plan owed much to this staff officer's gifts, the conception in its outline and pivotal points sprang direct from Allenby's own brain. Indeed, he had originally intended a less far-reaching manœuvre and a more limited envelopment. But, returning one day from a ride spent in reflection, he made the announcement, the more dramatic because of its crisp directness, that he had decided to sweep straight up the coastal plain to near Megiddo, cross by the passes into the Plain of Esdraelon — ancient Jezreel — and, by securing the road and rail centres of Afule and Beisan, block the Turkish lines of retreat, drawing tight the neck of a bag which contained this whole force.

I would suggest that the evolution of Allenby from the bad general of 1914–1915 into the great general of 1918 is less surprising than appears on the surface;

that the current can be traced throughout its course. For, as early as the Boer War, Allenby had shown an almost unique instinct for surprise and mobility, which the strange conditions of siege-warfare only damped but could not extinguish; they flickered into flame before Arras.

Perhaps even his impatience and irritability in France sprang from this forcible suppression of his natural instincts. The historian may also note two other influences of possible significance — the disappearance in Palestine of the neuritis in the arm from which Allenby had suffered throughout the winter of 1916–1917, and the death from wounds of his only son shortly after he left France. Hard experience awakened him to the reality of the changed conditions of warfare, widened his understanding of material factors, taught him that obstacles could not be changed until they had first been undermined, and in the hour of final illumination he was sent to a theatre of war which might have been designed by Providence for the display of his natural gifts, now refined by experience. If he had advanced to meet the new conditions of warfare, Palestine brought back these conditions as near as possible to meet him, and the convergence produced a military classic — perhaps the last masterpiece of the old warfare in its medium, the foreshadowing of the new in its technique, and a reassertion of the unchanging principles in its governing ideas.

Moreover, Allenby had passed not only to a military region of greater freedom — from barbed-wire entanglements — but into an atmosphere of greater freedom. In Palestine he was a supreme war-lord, not merely one of the "Barons," as the army commanders in France were somewhat aptly styled. And there is little doubt that he was cast by nature for an independent rôle, better and bigger in carrying out his own plans than in executing the orders of others; for although not insubordinate, subordination cramped and irked the free play of his genius and the full development of his powers. Experience and the change of conditions, both material and moral, combined to improve and expand him not only as a general but as a leader of men, to make him less of a martinet and more of a magnet, less intolerant and more understanding, less obstinate but no less resolute — in fact, to humanize "the Bull" whose coming many had feared, without diminishing but rather refining his inborn strength of character and purpose. Thus he not only achieved far greater results, but won far greater devotion.

In the Valley of Jezreel and the region of Megiddo Allenby wrote a glorious last chapter to the old testament of warfare. At Nazareth he wrote the preface to the new. And the scope of his achievement, like the faith he inspired, was due to the light that had come to him on his journey to Damascus.

HUNTER LIGGETT

A PROFESSOR OF WAR — AND HUMAN NATURE

HUNTER LIGGETT

A PROFESSOR OF WAR — AND HUMAN NATURE

AMONG all the Higher Commanders in France none looked less the part of great soldiers than the commanders of the First American Army and the Second British Army — Hunter Liggett and Herbert Plumer. A casual observer might have dismissed both with the remark that they were pleasant old gentlemen, so kindly and harmless that it was a shame to drag them from their firesides to such a grim and bloody ordeal. The men who served under them knew better, knew that their kindly demeanor was not a cloak for well-meaning incompetence, but the expression of minds fertilized by human understanding and ripened by experience to the knowledge that sympathy will draw an extra effort from sorely tried men when harshness will merely drive them to the breaking point. A new form of the old proverb that "manners makyth man." And with both these "pleasant old gentlemen" their troops also learned that this sympathy took the very practical form of an infinite care to safeguard the lives and well-being of the men in the fighting line. Each was blessed with a brilliant chief of staff — Harington with Plumer and Drum with Liggett—but the happy blend of their complementary qualities was yet another tribute to the personality of the Commander. And neither was overshadowed by his assistant.

Throughout nearly four years of war, Plumer's Second Army remained a symbol of confidence and contentment among the troops, enjoying an enviable and even unique reputation as an army in which all, if given the choice, would wish to serve. No higher tribute could be paid to a commander and staff than the practical recognition accorded during the Battle of Ypres, 1917. At the start, on July 31, the Second Army's share was limited to one corps on the fringe of the attack sector, but gradually, corps by corps, its control was extended until at the end it embraced almost the whole battle front. And although many reputations foundered in the swamps of Ypres and Passchendaele, even the hopeless conditions and inevitable losses of that field of fruitless sacrifice did not dim the troops' faith in Plumer.

If Liggett's test was less prolonged, it was hardly a less severe trial of his capacity and his men's confidence. To rise from command of a division in January 1918 to command of an army by October was in itself a searching test, but it was not the whole. For the American army, when it ultimately started, seemed to treat the war as a sprint race, and in going "all out" for the finishing tape gave short shrift to commanders who showed signs of failing to stand

From a photograph taken by a member of the Signal Corps

LIGGETT

the pace; whereas the other armies, after the opening sprint for victory had failed in 1914, settled down
to an attrition Marathon which gave more opportunity for leisurely examination of the runners' form.
Further, the strain of the hot pace set in the American army was increased by the condition of the
runners. It is a common remark that the United
States is the land of extremes, geographic, climatic,
social, psychological. Up to 1917 there was certainly
no more extreme contrast than that between the big
scale on which its commercial transactions were customarily conceived and conducted and the petty
scale of its military transactions. A pacific country,
its boast was of its big business and small forces,
but when plough- and other shares were converted
into swords, this characteristic contrast was a serious
handicap, and the mental expansion was perhaps
even more difficult than the material.

When the little 1914 British Expeditionary Force
of six divisions expanded to seventy, there was much
discussion as to the difficulty of handling such masses
with a General Staff which had been accustomed to
think in divisions, whereas the Continental General
Staffs had for decades thought in armies of millions.
But the American commanders and staffs had been
still more restricted in scope — brigades or battalions
were almost the limit of their ambition. And while
the British soldier had at least been trained in the
practical school of war by active service in many

colonial campaigns on a considerable scale, the American, as a rule, had spent his service in scattered garrisons in the homeland or, at most, a little punitive expedition against some insurgent tribe, such as the Moros, to vary the monotony. A lifetime of garrison duty and routine soldiering has an inevitable tendency to cramp the mind with each succeeding year thus passed, for such experience is no experience, in the true sense. One is reminded of the immortal story of Marshal Saxe and the aged general who based his claims to superior wisdom upon the number of his campaigns, whereupon Saxe pointed to a mule which had been through a score of campaigns but was "still a mule." In modern times, when command goes more than ever by seniority, the paralyzed grip of aged generals has been reflected in the increasing paralysis of war. And in 1917 the American army was no exception to this world-wide military rule of seniority, if all the more an exception to the civil rule that America was the land of youth and opportunity. Yet a survey of military history reveals the truth that "youth is surprise, and surprise is war." The roll of the Great Captains is not only a roll of youth for the main part, but it includes no man who spent long years in garrison duty. Among American soldiers, European military opinion recognizes the claims of Robert E. Lee and Stonewall Jackson to places in this roll.

In Lee's case, the Mexican War and engineering

work at Washington and Baltimore had given relief from the deadening influence of routine service. Stonewall Jackson was only twenty-seven when he abandoned the professional army to take up a professorship at Lexington. Ten years of study and quiet reflection enabled him to return with mind fresh and ungrooved, to conceive and execute the dazzlingly original moves of his ever-famous campaign in the Shenandoah Valley.

Why have I dwelt on these historical instances? Because they suggest a clue to Hunter Liggett's success, his ability to stay the course that found so many runners short of "wind." More perhaps than any other American military leader, he had kept mental age at bay by fulfilling Napoleon's maxim, "Read and re-read [the famous campaigns of military history]. That is the only way of becoming a great captain, to obtain the secret of the art of war."

Born at Reading, Pennsylvania, on March 21, 1857, and passing out from the U. S. Military Academy at West Point, in 1879, to a commission in the infantry, Hunter Liggett was then destined to spend the next thirty years in the humdrum activities of regimental soldiering, save for a few breaks. These included the Geronimo campaign against the Indians on the Mexican border, service on the adjutant-general's staff in the brief Spanish-American War of 1898, and a spell in the Philippines subsequently as major of volunteers. They were useful and character-forming interludes, but insufficient to offset the far longer periods of minor routine in a subordinate capacity. Character, moreover, is not often lacking among Anglo-Saxon soldiers, and the formation of character is apt to be a less urgent need than the formation of mind. It was a commonplace in 1914–1918 that among military leaders chins were more prominent than foreheads. And, on balance, the conditions of his service seemed to weight the scales heavily against Liggett, more heavily than against many of his contemporaries.

There is a significant contrast between the careers of the men who after a year of war service were given command of the First Army of their respective countries. Where Haig was a major general at forty-two, Liggett was still a regimental major at fifty-two. Surely no enthusiasm could survive such tardy promotion, no intellect rise above petty concerns after being confined so long within such narrow bounds of activity. But Liggett had preserved himself from stagnation by his interest in reading and in human nature. Like the military students of Europe, he had studied the campaigns of the nineteenth century, had become familiar with the French, German, and English authors who had sought to lay bare the methods of Napoleon and Moltke. But, unlike many of his comrades in the wideness of his reading, he was also unlike the majority of the European military students in extending his horizon to include earlier campaigns. By them Napoleon's first campaign was too commonly regarded as the Year One of military history. Liggett realized that the ancients also held out lessons of value. Few American soldiers would contend that professional education was carried to the pitch it had reached in France and Germany in the decades before the World War, but, if less intensive, Liggett at least could claim that his studies were more extensive than those of most of his European contemporaries.

The United States was even more belated than England in cultivating and encouraging the higher study of war, and not until Roosevelt's presidency was an Army War College established by Elihu Root. Even so, it was open several years before Liggett entered. He was fifty-two years of age and just promoted lieutenant colonel, but he soon showed that his mind was elastic enough to absorb instruction, and when he graduated next year he was appointed a director of studies at the College. At last his years of conscientious and solitary application to his profession had won recognition, and after three years in this capacity he was promoted brigadier general and appointed President of the Army War College in 1913. Too long had the American military outlook been that of the small-town tradesman of war; under Liggett's influence it was to begin developing the big-business sense. True, he could not provide the army corps of Continental Europe for the Higher

Commanders to practise with, but he could teach the budding commanders to think in army corps, and, to take the place of experience of handling large formations in the field, he introduced staff rides to study how these had been handled by the great leaders of the American Civil War. That war, after all, was a better education than any since Napoleon's, for whereas 1870 — to which French and German war colleges devoted so much attention — was chiefly a lesson in "how not to do it," the American Civil War was rich in examples of surprise and mobility, of unexpected thrusts, and skillful strategic combinations.

It was unfortunate for America that Liggett's stay at the War College was not longer, for in 1914 he was appointed to command the Fourth Brigade on the Mexican frontier. It is a popular but utterly false idea that men in the fighting line are more valuable than men on the staff, that a mass of uniformed men is synonymous with an army. Actually, the strength of any military force is in proportion to the strength of its foundations. The skyscrapers of New York are possible only because they are built on Manhattan rock; but Washington thought to build a skyscraper army in 1917 on sand, and in consequence a long and inevitable delay occurred while the fresh foundations of a staff were being laid in France.

Liggett was in Texas, anxiously watching the war cloud which hung threateningly over Mexico, when the greater storm broke in Europe, and it was characteristic of his quick perception of new military developments abroad that he put his men through a course of instruction in practical military engineering, the construction of trench lines and strong points, followed by attacks upon them. When the Mexican war cloud dispersed, he sailed for the Philippines, to command first a brigade and then the military department. In March 1917 he was promoted major general, and on the entry of the United States into the World War next month he returned to command the Western Department, with headquarters at San Francisco. All the summer he was busy in organizing the vast training camps which sprang up like mushrooms, but in September he was ordered to join the large party of generals which sailed for a tour of observation in France. If they went to inspect, they also went to be inspected, and many failed to survive the scrutiny of Pershing, the Commander in Chief.

The slow course of peace promotion in the United States army became a severe handicap under war conditions, and Pershing was dismayed at the age of the commanders first sent out. Liggett's handicap was "weight for age," for even his marked height was overshadowed by his girth, and his appearance created an inevitable impression that he was unsuited to the strain of active service. It would have been hard if all his width of study had now been wasted through his width of body. In a violent effort to overcome prejudice, he daily took strenuous walks. This proof of his activity, even coupled with his intellectual reputation, might not have sufficed but for the number of other "tourists" who were found unfit, mentally or physically. Orders actually came from the War Department for him to return home, if only temporarily, but Pershing asked leave to keep Liggett in place of another general of whom he was anxious to be rid. And, in reality, Liggett's appearance was delusive. General Bullard has testified to his tough physique, telling how he saw a horse fall with Liggett, "pitching him a great distance on a hard, rough road, from which he rose without sprain or injury."

He received command of the 41st Division, whose training he had supervised near San Francisco. This was assigned as a replacement, or draft-finding, division — a status which promised the commander little scope; but Liggett's personality as well as his theoretical knowledge proved a passport to promotion, and in January 1918 he was given command of the First American Army Corps, first in name and first to be formed. For the next six months, however, Liggett had a headquarters but hardly a command, as his divisions were first undergoing practical instruction in trench warfare under French tactical command and then, from April onward, were called on to help, piecemeal, in stopping the great German offensive. Many generals would have fretted impatiently over the delay, but not so Liggett. He was big enough mentally to realize that the Allied cause was greater than personal ambition, and that the period of waiting could be turned to profit by organizing the corps staff for its coming test. So, while his nominal divisions were fighting in front of Paris, — the 1st at Cantigny, the 2nd at Belleau Wood, — Liggett, in his headquarters at Neufchâteau in the Vosges, was quietly building up his conception of a model organization.

At last, on July 4, — significant date, — Liggett's 1st Corps took over a sector northwest of Château-Thierry, in the great Marne bulge made by the German offensive of May 27. Liggett had under him now the 26th American Division and the 167th French Division, with the 2nd American Division in reserve, and the mixed composition was continued by the fact that Liggett's Corps was part of Degoutte's Sixth French Army. This in turn formed with Mangin's Tenth Army the mass of manœuvre intended for Foch's great counterstroke against the western face of the Marne bulge. On July 15 the Germans launched their last offensive, on both sides of Rheims, the eastern bastion of the incurved line. They were stopped, if by a narrow margin, and on July 18 the counterstroke was delivered. The vital point was near Soissons, at the base of the German salient, where Mangin's penetration threatened to cut across the enemy's rear, and in the initial stage

Liggett's Corps was strategically part of the hinge for Mangin's advance. But when this began to be held up by the Germans, fighting desperately to keep open the neck of the salient to prevent their forces being cut off, Degoutte's army became the door instead of the hinge, swinging northward to clear the Germans from the salient. Thus the axis of advance from eastward became northeastward, involving a change of direction in difficult country. Liggett's initial advance had been as successful as any, and his troops had gone forward with great dash, but the change of direction proved too severe a test for the 26th Division, and one brigade had to be replaced by another from a fresh division. Nevertheless, his troops advanced faster than the tired French corps on his flanks, despite a long check at Sergy caused by fierce counterattacks, and they continued to share in the advance until August 13, when the Marne salient was cleared of the enemy. By that time three fresh American divisions and one more French had been used by Liggett.

This battle, the first time that an American army corps had been engaged since the Civil War, was an interesting début. The promise was actually more significant than the performance, for the average front of attack was only two and a half miles, and although its advance had covered twenty miles, it had only taken 674 prisoners and 7 guns for a loss of over 15,000 men in the American divisions alone —

a casualty toll which suggests that Liggett's instructions "to attack machine guns by envelopment and
never directly" had not been carried out. Such a
high proportion of loss, as the British had found in
1916, is the cost of unpreparedness, and must ever be
paid by new formations wherein gallantry is inborn
but skill a slow growth. One recalls Napoleon's
axiom: "With a raw army it is possible to carry a
formidable position, but not to carry out a plan or
design."

After its baptism of fire in the Second Battle of the
Marne, the 1st Army Corps was switched eastward
for the surprise stroke planned against the narrower
St. Mihiel salient, which during four years had been
an uncomfortable protuberance into the French front.
To cut away this tumor would not only relieve the
lateral rail arteries of the Allies but pave the way for
an advance toward Metz and the German communications. It was to be the first true American operation on a large scale. Liggett's 1st Corps and
Dickman's 4th Corps, each of four divisions, were to
deliver the main blow on the eastern face of the salient, while Cameron's 5th Corps, with one American
and one French division, struck the western face,
the two aiming to join hands across the base of the
salient and so cut off the German troops therein.
The success might have been greater if Liggett's
opinion had received more attention and had had
more influence. His sector was on the extreme

right, near the joint of the salient with the main front. For security he urged, but in vain, that he should be allowed to use a division to attack, not merely demonstrate against, the Vittonville ridges which overlooked the border of the actual salient, in order to prevent the enemy's artillery enfilading from this point the attack on the salient. For economy of force and lives, he insisted in his own Corps on the point that the front lines should be weak in numbers, with strong reserves well forward and always ready, but out of exposure. He did not find it easy to impress this principle on the divisional commanders, who were imbued with the fallacy — that their allies also had taken long to unlearn — of crowding men in the front lines as a target for the enemy's artillery. Thirdly, he argued against a long artillery preparation, on the ground that it cast away the essential element of surprise — but not with entire success, although the bombardment was short by the standards of 1916 and 1917. The repeated disregard of surprise — master key of all the Great Captains — is perhaps the most astounding feature of the generalship of 1914–1918. Liggett's early perception of the essential value of methods which the best of his allies only reached after years of trial and error, and which many of his contemporaries never arrived at, is a testimony to the superiority of study and reflection over mere experience, and to the value of a mind nourished on military history.

Although the Germans gained knowledge of the impending blow, they delayed a wise strategic retirement too long, and thus were caught by the attack in the course of their deliberate preparations, with part of their artillery withdrawn. The defenders were overwhelmed by four hours' intense bombardment from nearly 3000 guns, mostly French, and at 5 A.M. on September 12 the infantry and tanks advanced. Liggett had three divisions leading, with one in reserve, and before midday they had reached their final objectives, quicker than was anticipated, owing to the free rein given by Liggett's instruction that units should press on as long as possible, without checking to keep alignment with their neighbors, so long as their flanks were not unduly exposed.

Dazed and without artillery support, the Germans offered practically no resistance, but Liggett asked permission in vain to make a further bound, which would have ruptured the German line, the Michel Stellung, across the base of the salient. The 4th Corps on his left and the 5th Corps opposite, which by converging were to cut off the Germans in the apex of the salient, gained their objectives with equal ease, but, tied too strictly to the apron strings of the Higher Command, they halted to await further orders. Pershing's orders for them to continue were slow to reach the troops; they did not arrive until after dark; and thus the bulk of the Germans had slipped through and safely away before the two Corps

joined hands next morning. These Corps then
wheeled north and up into alignment with the 1st
Corps, facing the Michel Stellung, by the 15th, when
the battle was broken off. The only serious fighting
had been borne by the 1st Corps, which had met with
counterattacks owing to the menacing direction which
its advance had taken; the enemy was willing to
evacuate the salient, but he had no intention of letting
his base line be crossed if he could prevent it. The
1st Corps also suffered loss from enfilading by artillery from Vittonville, as Liggett had foreseen. Even
so, the loss of the 1st Corps was less than its tally of
prisoners, 5000; and the total American casualties
were less than half the total prisoners. If a sledge
hammer had been used to crush a bubble, and the
exploitation had fallen short, a success so economical
was an inestimable tonic to a new army, and that,
after all, was an underlying purpose of the St. Mihiel
offensive.

The American army had undergone its trial run;
it was now to enter the race for victory as the right
wing of the converging Allied advance against the
Germans' main lateral railway and their exits of
retreat on either side of the Ardennes. Immediately
after the curtain was rung down on the St. Mihiel
attack, the American striking forces were shifted
westward to the sector between the river Meuse and
the Argonne Forest. They had scarcely a week of
preparation, an astonishing contrast with the months

of preparation which had preceded the British Somme offensive of 1916, and even though the German fighting power and morale were now vastly different, such haste put an almost superhuman strain on new troops with a new organization. Popular opinion might complain of the number of breakdowns; the military critic can only marvel that there were not more, and that complete collapse did not come.

Of the three American corps sectors, Liggett's Corps was assigned the left, which lay in the Argonne Forest, and the difficulty of its task was enhanced by the fact that this obstacle was not inclusive to it, but shared with a French corps on the western flank. Such a division of responsibility violated all military principles, hindering the coördination of the attacks on both flanks of the forest. Nevertheless, the opening of the offensive was rich in promise. The American attackers were only brought up at the last moment to pass through the French screen holding the trenches, a complete surprise was scored, and with twelve divisions against five German divisions less than half their strength, — a superiority of fully five to one, — a great success seemed within reach. And this American blow was aimed at the most sensitive point of the German front, with less than thirty miles to go in order to reach the vital lateral railway. Unhappily, the centre Corps — the 5th — which had its flanks protected, did less well than its neighbors who had the more difficult task and ground. On the

1st Corps' front, Liggett's orders paved the way for a good start. Thus the formidable obstacle of Vauquois was neatly circumvented by an encircling advance, instead of a direct assault, and the initial impetus drove a wedge nearly four miles deep up the Aire valley east of the Argonne.

Then a brake was put on the advance by Pershing's orders for a halt on reaching the Corps' objective, and it was difficult to get up momentum again after six hours' delay. A method that was sound in siege warfare was, as Liggett's insight told him, a mistake when faced with a weak and temporarily demoralized enemy. The Americans had, as yet, neither the training nor the organization for methodical siege-warfare operations, and the best chance of decisive success lay in swamping the defense by a human torrent in the first flush of surprise, before the enemy could bring up reënforcements. With the brake put on prematurely, the advance thereafter slowed down and became spasmodic. Guns could not get forward to support the infantry, control lapsed, and supplies not infrequently failed, through inexperience accentuating the natural difficulties of the ground. The arrival of fresh German divisions enabled the enemy to counterattack and force back the disjointed attackers in places. A renewed general attack on October 4 made little progress and revealed once more the folly of trying to overthrow machine guns by sheer weight of human bodies, without adequate support or surprise. But the value of training was also shown by the regular 1st Division in Liggett's Corps, which drove in a deep if narrow wedge on the east bank of the Aire. This enabled Liggett, on October 7, to try a manœuvre both original and daring: bringing the 82nd Division up in the wake of the 1st, he swung it against the enemy's flank west of the Aire and then northward. If the execution fell below the conception, — only a tithe of the division came into action, — so that the chance of cutting off the enemy troops in the Argonne was lost, the threat at least persuaded the enemy to retire from the forest while there was time, and by October 10 the American line had passed and was clear of this hampering obstacle.

Two days later Liggett was summoned to take command of the First American Army, the whole force engaged in the offensive. The promotion was all the greater tribute because it came at a time when commanders of all grades were falling beneath the sickle of dismissal almost as fast as their men beneath the scythe of the enemy machine guns.

His appointment was too late for him to have any influence on the next general attack of October 14, already planned and ordered. This achieved little, at large cost, and with its failure the Meuse-Argonne offensive had run itself to a standstill. An attempt to press on, with exhausted troops and disordered communications, could exercise no pressure adequate to be any appreciably greater relief to the other Allied armies. Moreover, the British left wing of the Allied offensive, in which the 27th and 30th American Divisions shared, had already broken through the last defenses of the Hindenburg Line, and by October 5 had emerged into open country, with only natural obstacles, mileage, and a devastated area to hinder its advance.

The First American Army was closer to a vital point, and if it could have leaped forward in mid-October might have cut off the retreat of a large part of the German armies. But such a rapid bound was out of the question, and Liggett was wise enough to realize that in the circumstances it was far better to rest and reorganize his forces for a sure bound, as soon as possible, than to sacrifice lives in attempting the impossible. While utilizing the breathing space not only to replenish his ranks and supplies but to improve his communications and overhaul his organization, he carried out local operations to obtain a good jumping-off line for the fresh bound. Further, he recast the plan. Pershing had proposed that the American left should strike first, followed in turn by the remaining Corps to the right. This meant battering first at the naturally strong and heavily wooded Bois de Bourgogne area due north of the Argonne, where also the enemy were in strongest force. Liggett preferred to drive a broad wedge in the centre and so outflank the Bois de Bourgogne area, threatening its encirclement in conjunction with the advance of the French Fourth Army to the west.

It was well conceived, for, when Liggett unleashed his forces on November 1, this area was the only one which showed resisting power, and by next day the enemy rearguards there had disappeared and were falling back as fast as on the rest of the American front. If the Germans were offering little resistance, the very rapidity of the pursuit — outstripping the French on the flank — imposed almost as great a strain, and it was a tribute to Liggett's preparations that the First Army machine functioned much more smoothly than in the earlier phase. And this despite the execution of a most difficult manœuvre, by which the whole Army wheeled progressively to the right during the course of the pursuit, ready for an attack northeastwards, — against the strong position between the Meuse and Chiers rivers to which the enemy had retired, — as a preliminary to an advance towards Metz, if the Armistice had not rung down the curtain.

The historian who scans the whole horizon of the war must recognize that this last offensive, beginning on November 1, had only a minor influence, for Ludendorff had fallen from power, his pleas for a renewed stand on the German frontier rejected, and the enemy were already suing for peace before Liggett struck. And the potential threat of a thrust through Lorraine by the newly assembled Franco-American mass of manœuvre was a greater urge not to quibble over the Armistice terms than the advance on the Meuse, which, like the rest of the original Allied offensive, was difficult to maintain without a halt to repair the communications, and from whose embrace the Germans had by now slipped away at the sacrifice of their rearguards. Nevertheless, it was well that the Armistice had tarried long enough to allow the offensive of November 1 to take place, if only as a counterpoise to the bitter memories of the first phase of the Meuse-Argonne, and a proof that, when purged and refined by experience, the American army could produce leadership and staff work worthy of the gallant sacrifice of the fighting troops — the American nation in arms.

When the First Army was disbanded after the Armistice, Liggett passed to the command of the Third Army — of occupation — in Germany, until July 1919, when he returned home, to settle down in San Francisco, in the heart of the state whose citizens he had prepared in 1917 for their ordeal by battle. They at least showed an appreciation of his services, a delight in appropriating as their own one whom they reverenced not merely for his work but for his character. But a grateful country, or rather its Government, reverting to the peace-time tradition of indifference, automatically demoted him to the rank of major general which he had held before the war, letting him retire on the same pittance as the scores

of routine-minded commanders — in name only —
whose shallowness of character and knowledge had
been exposed under the test of war.

If the proverb be true, "Ingratitude to their great
men is the mark of strong peoples," the American
nation must surely be the strongest people on earth.

Not that Liggett worried. It would have been
appropriate if he had settled down in retirement not
in San Francisco but in Cincinnati, for he was of the
type of the historic Roman leader who could lay down
the insignia of power and retire to his farm, content
with his own sense of duty well done. While his
power of command and study earned him respect,
his simplicity and kindliness evoked affection — they
are the qualities to which the men who served him
in all grades instinctively pay first tribute. He had
the faith of the soldier in Balzac's "Christ in Flanders." Single-minded and high-minded, giving and
receiving trust, he was a pattern of the traditional
military virtues. But he achieved a reconciliation
far from common between spirit and mind : as he
was distinguished from this simple type by his
breadth of study, so he was distinguished from the
typical academic soldier by his understanding of
human nature.

"BLACK JACK" PERSHING

THE "100–PER–CENT AMERICAN"

"BLACK JACK" PERSHING

THE "100-PER-CENT AMERICAN"

THE phrase "100-per-cent American" has become both a description and a motto since the war. If General Pershing was not the prototype, he deserves to be — for it fits aptly both as a description of him and as a motto for him.

Born on September 13, 1860, near Laclede, Missouri, John Joseph Pershing was destined to as astonishing a rise from the nadir of lowliness to the zenith of power as Joffre, first commander in chief of the other great republic. And like Joffre, this product of democracy was essentially undemocratic. His early years were a perfect fulfillment of the popular picture of the self-made man — as a boy, improving his education in hours snatched from work, then taking a course at the Normal School at Kirksville while supporting himself by teaching in a children's school. Law was his aim, but arms his fate, for, hearing of a competitive examination for the United States Military Academy at West Point, he turned aside to try for, and seize, the chance of a career free of apprenticeship costs. If the prize seemed likely to be small, the stake was nought.

More mature than most of the cadets, with the habit of command already ingrained through his teaching experience, he was elected president of his class as a freshman, then selected by his officers as corporal after a year, first sergeant the next, and in his last year first captain in the Corps of Cadets. These appointments were proofs more of character than of book knowledge. Physically tough, morally hard, he had come out on top in a rough-and-tumble school of youth, and he inspired more respect than affection. Even when, on graduating, he attained the dignity of commissioned rank, he did not hesitate to cure one case of insubordination with his fists. This, like the incident when, as a general on the pursuit of Villa, he pushed his way into the mess line among the soldiers for a plate of beans and cup of coffee, was later glorified as an instance of democratic habits. In reality it was merely an example of his unceremonious way of going straight for what he wanted by the shortest route and regardless of other people.

This unceremonious, or self-centred, instinct remained with him when he became a world figure and created many shocks in the politer atmosphere of Europe, where opinions might be as frank but were less so in expression. There were times when the language barrier was of value as a buffer. Even in smaller matters Pershing's ways were disconcerting. His disregard of time and appointments was proverbial. If he arranged to dine with one of the Allied commanders in chief, he thought nothing of keeping him waiting for hours. Pétain, fortunately, came to regard him as an interesting and highly original object for study, while Haig merely went on with his meal. Again, at a ceremonial arrival at a station, — Bucharest, it is said, — where royalty was waiting on the platform to greet him, Pershing was seen by the horrified station master to be in shirt sleeves, shaving. With a promptness which stamped him as a born diplomatist the station master ordered the train to be backed out until Pershing had completed his toilet.

Yet, if a "rough diamond," in his cadet days at West Point as in France later he had one aspect in curious and softened contrast — his love of dancing and of dances.

Graduating from West Point in 1886, he was commissioned in the Cavalry and passed almost directly to active service in the campaign against Geronimo, the notorious Apache chief, wherein he earned a mention in dispatches. Henceforward he was to take part in many of those little guerrilla campaigns which were the American officer's sole practical training for the command of the vast forces of 1918, and to win more commendations than any of his contemporaries. Pershing, however, had one interlude of a different nature. After heading a rescue party to save some cowboys from the Indians in 1889 and being in charge of Indian scouts in the Sioux rising of 1890, he retired for four years to the more peaceful occupation of being military instructor at the University of Nebraska, and utilized his spare time to graduate from the law school. At the outbreak of the Spanish-American War he was back again at West Point as an assistant instructor, but resigned in order to serve with a cavalry regiment in Cuba, where he not only won more "mentions" but attracted the attention of Theodore Roosevelt and drew this tribute from his Commander: "I have been in many fights, through the Civil War, but Captain Pershing is the coolest man under fire I ever saw in my life." Twenty years later a member of Congress cast the slur that he had never seen Pershing within sixty miles of the front in France — an imputation that was hotly resented by many who had seen Pershing at the front and knew the difficulty which his staff had met in trying to hold him back from unnecessary exposure.

With the end of the Spanish-American War, Pershing had a chance to show that he possessed more qualities than mere bravery and energy. Sent to the Philippines, he found time from the trivial job of commanding a troop of cavalry to study the ways of the Moros, a savage and fanatical tribe of Mohammedans who were the terror of Mindanao and regarded as too intractable ever to civilize. His association with them and interest in a matter outside the beaten paths of routine caused jealousy and disapproval among his fellows — until an emergency came. Then this mere captain was called to take a general's rôle and to be not only military commander but administrator of the district where lay the Moro country. By the blend of military force with diplomacy and unexpected sympathy, helped greatly by the fact that he could negotiate with the Moros without the intervention of an interpreter, he brought order into that turbulent country. President Roosevelt paid him the rare tribute of citing his name in a message to Congress, and sought to find a loophole in the hard and fast regulations by which he could be given special promotion. To change regulations is hard enough, but this required the passing of new legislation in Congress, and in the meanwhile Pershing went out as military attaché to Tokyo. He was just in time for the Russo-Japanese War and was promptly detailed to accompany the Japanese forces in Manchuria, enduring the mortification of being a captain forty-four years of age among foreign generals hardly his senior.

But at last Roosevelt, tired of waiting for the slow machinery of Congress to enable him to give Pershing a step up the ladder of promotion, used his power of creating brigadier generals, but no less, to raise Pershing at a bound to this exalted rank — over the heads of eight hundred and sixty-two of his seniors. It was another example of the common experience, in England as in America, that the only hope of radical reform in the military forces lies in the chance of a dominating personality, seriously interested in military progress, as the political chief — the soldier chiefs have rarely the instinct or the power to break the entwining coils of red tape.

Pershing's jump in promotion naturally caused widespread jealousy, which found an explanation satisfying to its meanness in the fact that before sailing for Japan Pershing had married the daughter of Senator Warren of Wyoming, chairman of the Senate Committee on Military Affairs. It was conveniently overlooked that he had not even met his future bride at the time President Roosevelt cited his services in the message to Congress. Nevertheless the innuendoes were so general that Roosevelt found it necessary to intervene with a statement that "to promote a man because he married a senator's daughter would be infamy; to refuse him promotion for the same reason would be equal infamy."

On his promotion Pershing returned to the Philippines as commander of the department of Mindanao and governor of the Moro province — there to complete his work of subjugation and reconciliation. From the Philippines he passed to the command of a brigade at San Francisco, but when trouble developed on the Mexican border his record made it natural that he should be sent thither. While absent on this duty a disastrous fire broke out in the Presidio, the military headquarters at San Francisco, in which his wife and three daughters lost their lives. It was well for him that duty soon called him to an arduous task in which he could work off his emotion. This was the punitive expedition into Mexico in pursuit of the bandit leader Villa, who had crossed and ravaged the American border. Hampered by the difficulties of the country and obstructed by Carranza's nominal government, Pershing's strenuous and relentless pursuit was finally frustrated by his own government, and on President Wilson's orders he had first to halt and then to withdraw. In such a country such a wavering attitude not only encouraged defiance but imposed an unfair strain on the military commander. But a marked feature of Pershing throughout his career was a loyal and unquestioning acceptance of the dictates, however incomprehensible and irritating, of his superiors. Few would have accepted a task almost foredoomed to failure by its restricting conditions, but Pershing's instinct of obedience was so absolute that he gave the impression that he would sacrifice anything, even his men, rather than disobey an order.

As he was a man of undeniable ambition, this rigid subordination of himself, uncommon among men of such strong personality, probably sprang less from belief in the infallibility of authority than from a farsighted wisdom — smoothing the way for his own ascent. His combined tractability and efficiency won him favor in the eyes of President Wilson.

Promoted major general, Pershing was appointed early in 1917 to succeed, on the death of Funston, to the supreme command on the Mexican border. And in May, after the entry of the United States into the World War, the President announced that Pershing was to go to Europe in command of the American forces. It was to be a dramatic change, particularly in scale, from his previous experience. To pass from guerrilla expeditions in jungle, mountain, and desert to the vast siege in progress — or stagnation — on the French front was a contrast so utter as to leave him destitute of any foundation of knowledge on which to build.

Fortunately he had partaken of other kinds of experience — building roads and schools in the jungle, maintaining a line of communications in hostile territory, bringing order into the disorder of a land occupied by an obstinate and insurgent people.

However different in degree from his new task, this experience had made him a trained administrator; he had acquired the habit of organization with the will and knack to get his plans carried into effect. There is even some ground for the verdict that his unmilitary experience had fitted him for the command in France as much as his military experience had unfitted him.

At the end of May, Pershing sailed for France on the Baltic with the nucleus of his newly gathered staff, leaving a semiparalyzed War Department,

From the War Album of " L'Illustration "

PERSHING DISEMBARKING IN FRANCE

clogged by its own antiquated machinery and over-whelmed by its unforeseen responsibility, to send on material enough to build a shanty while he was erect-ing the framework of a military skyscraper. To chide the home authorities for their inadequate and dilatory measures might only lead to the wreck of his dream and the downfall of himself. It was better that the pressure on them should come gradually from public opinion, growing uneasy over the delay, than from him; meanwhile the Allies must do their best to hold the pass. The latter had imagined that the United States would produce troops in the manner of a conjurer producing rabbits from his hat; instead they found Pershing ploughing the soil and sowing seeds with all the deliberation of a Middle-West farmer who reckons in months, not in hours, waiting tran-quilly for the ultimate ripening of his crops. If they were disconcerted by the contrast between their con-ception of their new ally as a high-speed "hustler" and the extreme deliberation which they found to be the reality, it was partly because they did not realize the difference between raising an army and using a navy already in existence, and partly because of the difference of outlook and temperament between a General Pershing and an Admiral Sims. If Sims's object was to win the war anyhow, Pershing's was, so it seemed, to win it with an American army stamped with the Pershing seal. If personal ambi-tion was a factor, there are side lights which suggest loftier and more far-reaching motives — to hand down to his country a tradition of military pride, to awaken her to a realization of her own power, to establish the permanent foundations of a national army.

When he settled down to his task after the arrival celebrations were over, — an infliction personally distasteful which he had accepted in deference to the French desire to gain the full benefit of this moral tonic, — he early revealed the keynotes of his policy. It is interesting to recall the impression he made upon his new Chief of Staff, Harbord. "He is very patient and philosophic under delays from the War Department" — although it took days and even weeks to get a reply to his cables and even to pass them from one branch to another of that archaic establishment. "He is playing for high stakes and does not intend to jeopardize them by wasting his standing with the War Department over small things." Further, the Chief of Staff found him "very cautious" and concerned with detail to such an extent as to edit and alter every cable and letter that was put to him for signature. "It is a good precaution, but one which can easily be carried to a point where it will waste time better employed on bigger things." But, as evidence from every quarter confirms, "his great fault is the utter lack of any idea of time" — time-blind as others are color-blind. If his concern with detail, most marked in the early stages, was partly

inspired by his aim of getting all his staff to think
and act as replicas of himself, in order that when the
hour of trial came he might be freed from detail, his
lack of sense of time was prejudicial to his own policy.
For allies could not but feel that a man who arrived
casually at midnight for a dinner fixed at six o'clock
would be likely to arrive on the battlefield when the
battle was lost. This feeling inevitably led them to
question arguments of his for going "slow but sure"
which were outwardly sound; and by creating jus-
tifiable uneasiness this defect increased friction,
whereas the very incompatibility of his policy with
the Allies' immediate needs urged the need of diminishing the other and unnecessary causes of friction.
That, despite this, Pershing carried his policy through
is a testimony to the strength and force of his character — all the more because he had to deal with men
also strong and stubborn in the Allied armies.

√ When Clemenceau sent a hint, for dissemination,
to the French Ambassador at Washington that Pershing and Pétain did not get on well, Pershing, hearing
of it, wrote direct to Clemenceau, telling him bluntly
that he had spread a wrong impression. This rebuke
from a mere soldier to the chief of an allied state,
especially when that chief was Clemenceau, deserves
to go on record as one of the boldest acts of the war.
Bearding the Tiger might well replace the familiar
phrase about "bearding the lion in his den."

And, with all his caution toward Washington,

Pershing did not fear responsibility. Harbord tells how, not long after his arrival, he placed an order for $50,000,000 worth of aircraft without obtaining authority, because he thought Washington was too slow. It is a further side light on his methods that he did not cable a word of having given this order until it was too late for Washington to countermand it. Similarly, his cable of July 6, 1917, "Plans should contemplate sending over at least a million men by next May," and his full project of July 11 which visualized an ultimate expansion to three million, were severe jolts to the War Department, still thinking of a limited-liability war.

The work of building the organization for the army of his vision was a stern test both of Pershing and of his judgment in choosing men — an essential quality in a great leader. As Harbord aptly remarked: "Officers whose lives have been spent in trying to avoid spending fifteen cents of government money now confront the necessity of expending . . . millions of dollars — and on their intellectual and professional expansion depends their avoidance of the scrap heap." Pershing's achievement was a tribute not merely to himself but to America — that its atmosphere, or its geography, breeds men with the habit of thinking "big" and with a mental elasticity that can survive even the restrictions which its army life imposes.

Pershing, unlike other famous commanders, was

neither a puppet in the hands of a clever staff nor an artist of war relieved of organizing cares by technical experts so that his mind might dwell in contemplation of what Saxe termed "the sublime branches of the art of war." Pershing had proved himself an organizer and administrator in the Philippines and in Mexico, yet even so the quickness with which his mind expanded to the scale of the World War is a greater miracle than the war expansion of America, which was full of men accustomed by their civil training to "big business." And if, when the foundations were laid, he handed over the execution to others, while retaining control, he was but fulfilling the principle on which alone a great organization, once started, can be run. If he gave his subordinates shorter shrift than in the armies of the Allies, he also gave them a freer hand while they held their posts. If this method led to mistakes, it also sifted the grain from the chaff in quick time.

Moreover, he had a real knack in picking his men and a catholicity of selection unusual in the professional soldier. If the choice of Dawes, one of history's most versatile handy men, as purchasing agent of all supplies for the American forces, and later as member and moving spirit of the Military Board of Allied Supply, was the most apt example, Pershing's utilization of the brains of some of the younger professional soldiers in important staff appointments was almost as notable. So also was the use he made of

Robert Bacon — former banker, Secretary of State, and ambassador — as his personal liaison officer, for Bacon did more than almost any man to oil the grating machinery of the Allied armies. This friction, often intense, was inevitable because of the difficulty of reconciling Pershing's policy and America's interests with the immediate interests of her allies. It is absurd to pretend that the motives of any nation are inspired purely by quixotic chivalry. Even in the best, honor and self-interest are mingled, and their rulers would be unworthy of their responsibility if it were otherwise. If in August 1914 many in England called for war out of loyalty to the Entente, and would have gone to the aid of France even if their country had held back, as did numerous Americans; if the mass of England's citizens in taking up arms thought of nothing beyond the pledge to safeguard outraged Belgium and preferred war to the forfeit of their honor — even this is a lofty and enlightened form of self-interest; there is, nevertheless, no question that the wiser heads realized with equal force the menace of a triumphant Germany.

Honor, prestige, prosperity — who can disentangle them? Thus in 1917–1918, if it was natural that France and England, strained almost beyond endurance, should urge that the American drafts be infused into their depleted ranks, and logical that such a combination of new blood and a tried organization would give quicker results, it was also natural that America should decline to lose her identity and sacrifice her national pride by such a merging — tacit avowal of inferiority. And Pershing could also counter logic with a proverb rooted in experience, that "no man putteth new wine into old bottles; else the new wine will burst the bottles, and be spilled." Troops will endure much mishandling from commanders of their own nationality, but patience is soon strained when things go wrong under a foreign command. If America's allies had reason on their side in this controversy, Pershing had human nature on his, in claiming that American troops should be under American command.

In the study of Pershing's uncompromising advance toward his own goal lies the main historical interest of his first year in France. Grant is held up as history's great example of a man who, having fixed his goal in his own mind, pursued it unswervingly and with almost unique pertinacity despite all obstacles — and without hesitating over the cost. Pershing, who had other points of resemblance to Grant, maintained his purpose with a determination at least equal to that of Grant, and under difficulties greater in all respects save only that Grant had to drive a tired, Pershing a fresh, steed. Where Grant had a Lincoln behind him, Pershing had far less resolute and clear-sighted support. And Grant had no allies to complicate his problem. A cynic might even say that the war for Pershing consisted of fifteen months' fighting at the rear and two months' fighting at the front.

The first storm signals were hoisted when Joffre, in the flush of his triumphant tour of the United States which coincided with America's entry, was named to "collaborate" with Pershing. The French had conceived the idea of rejuvenating their exhausted military body by grafting on the gland of America's youth, an operation that would have the advantage of putting an old head on young shoulders, if incidentally it would also contribute to French prestige. Soon after Pershing's arrival in France, Joffre and his entourage made their appearance at Pershing's headquarters, to be welcomed as honored guests. If this treatment appeared to satisfy Joffre, his staff soon showed that they had expected less honor and more consultation, to become part of the family, not merely guests, and began to ask when the collaboration was to be discussed. But Pershing had "no thought of engaging any nurse for himself, not even so eminent a one as Joffre." When this attempt at "infiltration" was seen to be a failure, the French began a series of more direct advances, reënforced by the fact that they had to supply so much of the material to equip the American troops and even their training camps and schools, which seemed to establish some claim to a voice in the control.

It may be thought, in view of subsequent troubles

in repeating the mistakes made by their allies in 1914–1916, that the American leaders were too chary in accepting advice based on experience, but it may also be said that the French would have been wiser not to push their opinions so forcibly down American throats. Most of the Americans came to France willing to learn, but they were sensitive to the suspicion of being patronized. The British, in France at least, seem to have been wiser, or more reserved, and usually waited until their advice was sought.

But the suspicion of patronage was accentuated by the still stronger suspicion of the object behind it — that of merging the American troops in the French army, and so bringing to nought Pershing's dream of a great American army striking the decisive blow. He was willing to examine the French and British systems, to take from each points that he liked, but the finished model was to be definitely American, for good or ill.

With a conflict of aims between two such strong men and blunt speakers as Pétain and Pershing, an explosion had to come before a settlement was possible. Despite polite rebuffs and obvious hints that they were unwanted, the French strove to keep a finger in the pie by creating numberless "missions," until Pershing, losing patience, gave an unmistakable warning of the futility of their efforts by a peremptory refusal of the offer to give him a tactical adviser. It was then that a new method of indirect attack was tried, instanced in Pétain's criticisms to Colonel House of the American system of training and in Clemenceau's letter to Washington. All failed against Pershing's solid front; but if Pershing and Pétain came gradually to respect each other's determination, bickering between the staffs was not extinct.

The British hardly came into the tussle until later; they were not in need of man-power until after the campaign of 1917, when they had exhausted themselves in maintaining the war almost single-handed. The British Government, with the submarine danger past its worst, then offered to supply the ships to bring over one hundred and fifty battalions to be trained and merged in the British forces. General Tasker Bliss, the American member of the military committee of the Supreme War Council, was in favor of this scheme, but Pershing was only willing to use it as a means to his end, and stipulated that complete divisions should be brought over. Despite the gloomy prediction of his allies, his own view was that "nothing yet justifies our relinquishment of our firm purpose to form our own army under our own flag. . . . There is no reason for scattering them among the Allies as divisions, much less as replacements, except in a crisis of sheer necessity." That crisis came sooner than he anticipated. The haze of discussion was swept away by the sudden blast of the German offensive on March 21. Faced

with the imminence of disaster, Pershing not merely
accepted the supreme command of Foch, with the
President's approval, but in the generous emotion of
the moment offered him the use of the American
troops in France to dispose as he willed, unlimited by
any conditions — perhaps realizing that in pursuit
of his ideal he had underrated the immediate reality
and risked the issue of the war. At the end of
March there were five American divisions in France,
but in response to the urgent and united appeal of
the Allies the dispatch of troops was raised to 300,000
a month — nearly as many as had arrived during the
previous twelve months.

This mood of Pershing's passed sooner than the
crisis. Lord Reading had obtained from the Washington authorities a promise to send over only
infantry and machine-gunners — liquid cement to
fill the ominous cracks in the Western Front.
Pershing demurred, and as a result of a conference
with Lord Milner, the Secretary of State for War,
arranged that this stream should only continue until
May, and thereafter be regulated to a flow of organized divisions. Happily, by then the worst danger
was averted, however narrowly, and Pershing's
ideal could develop unchecked into a reality.

His principle of a separate and independent
American army was related to another, the two forming the twin pillars of his policy. This second principle, a tactical one, was that of training his men for

a war of movement with the rifle as the dominant weapon. The historian may feel less certain that on this point Pershing was serving the interests of his country. Pershing, and most of his officers, bred on open fighting, were aghast at the way in which the other armies, especially the French, had become immersed in trench warfare. Bred also on the rifle, they ascribed this immersion not to its true cause, the battlefield mastery of the machine gun, but to the excessive use of grenades and other trench weapons, and were confirmed in this opinion by the efforts that they found were being made by the British Command to develop the use of the rifle afresh. This appeared to them much more significant than the development of the tank, which might be regarded as merely another trench-warfare device.

Further, they connected the loss of offensive spirit, which they found so marked among the French, with the prevalence of trench warfare and of trench weapons. Both assumptions were true in part, but only the lesser part. For trench warfare and trench weapons had arisen because riflemen could no longer make headway against machine guns.

Inspired by the right idea, but based on false premises, Pershing established the cult of the rifle in the new American army. And believing that it was possible to break through the trench front, given troops full of the offensive spirit, he trained his men for open warfare and attack with all the fervor which the French had shown before 1914. He realized that it would mean heavy sacrifices, but he felt that he had an ample draft of man-power to stake with — so had the French in 1914. In his advocacy of what was sometimes termed the "Brusiloff system," — getting men killed in order to get the war over quickly, — he did not appreciate that Russia, France, and Britain had all held the same faith; the first was now bankrupt, the second almost, and the third severely shaken. It was fortunate for Pershing that he had to face the Germans of 1918, not of 1914. If his policy was based on a balanced appreciation of this difference he could claim to be justified by the result, yet fate had an ironical last word, for he thereby thwarted the aim of his own policy of striking the decisive blow, in 1919, with an American army of his own creation taking the major share in the overthrow of the enemy.

His emphasis on the rifle and his belief that victory in modern war could be won by weight of infantry were to have a marked influence on his strategy in the day when at last he was able to turn from organization to command in battle. In the sphere of strategy he thought clearly and directly, if not deeply, and his choice of the ultimate American battleground was fixed in his mind soon after his arrival in France. The British were committed to operations in Flanders and northeastern France, an area which for all its handicaps — mud especially — was nearest to their home base and gave them the shortest line of communications through the Channel ports. The French offensive operations had all been conducted in the sector in front of Paris, and it was natural that they should concentrate to cover this vital centre. But the easterly sector facing and flanking Metz was obviously the Germans' most sensitive point, because a thrust there had only a short distance to penetrate before it imperiled the whole German front in France — by cutting the eastern end of the great lateral railway from Metz to Maubeuge and closing the Germans' exit of retreat east of the wooded Ardennes region. Moreover, it promised the vital economic effect of releasing the Briey iron region and threatening the Saar basin, upon which the enemy largely depended for his munitions. The choice of this sector, too, was the natural one for the Americans, because it clashed least with their allies' lines of communication and was easiest of access from their base ports in southwestern France.

Pershing had long to wait before his project could mature. On May 28 the 1st Division came into action at Cantigny, to cut the first notch of its splendid tally; early in June the 2nd Division at Château-Thierry helped to cement the breach made by the enemy's great drive to the Marne; in July and August nine American divisions took part in the counterstroke which marked the tilting of the scales on the Western Front. At last Pershing was able to summon back most of his scattered divisions to engage in the first All-American operation — the reduction of the St. Mihiel salient. Characteristically he made more than ample provision of force for the task. He was right to do so, for a failure would have been a moral disaster, and would have been hailed by the critics as pricking the bubble of his presumption in insisting upon independent command. Prepared with great care and with a secrecy remarkable in a raw army, delivered with a great superiority of force, both in American infantry and in French guns, the converging blow achieved its geographical object of pinching out the salient. If it failed to cut off the retreat of the enemy in the salient, it was not the first Allied stroke which had failed, through delay in orders and blocks behind the front, to reap the material fruits of success.

The strategic exploitation was a bigger issue. Pershing, with forces far larger than he needed for the task and composed of tried divisions, had wished to make the capture of the St. Mihiel salient a stepping stone to an advance toward Metz and the German rear flank. He gained Foch's agreement and the Allied Commander in Chief framed a plan whereby the British were to attack the Hindenburg Line and advance northeast toward Maubeuge, the French to push northward from Champagne, while the Americans were striking northeastward through Metz. Haig strongly disagreed with this divergent direction of advance and urged that it was essential that all attacks should converge on the main German armies so that each might react more closely on the others. He persuaded Foch to this view, and accordingly the American sector of advance was changed to the Meuse-Argonne, where it would be nearest to the great lateral railway through Mézières and Sedan. Thus the St. Mihiel attack was strictly limited to the reduction of the salient, and Pershing even felt bound by his instructions, from Foch, to refuse Liggett's 1st Corps permission to exploit their opening success by advancing against the Michel Stellung, the base line of the salient.

This strategic tug of war between Haig and Pershing, with Foch as the rope, is not easy to judge. It is an obvious principle that a converging attack has greater chances and is more likely to produce immediate results than a diverging attack. Thus Haig had justification in military principles as well as in the need to ease the formidable task of the British in assaulting the ill-famed Hindenburg Line. But Pershing could argue that he was fulfilling the Napoleonic method of thrusting at the enemy's rear, and that success here might have a still more far-reaching effect than a converging advance. It depended, however, on a penetration far deeper and swifter than any yet imagined on the Western Front, and with an untried army this was surely a remote hope. Pershing would seem in this matter, as over the rifle, to have placed more reliance on faith and tradition than on experience.

The outcome was contrary to both opinions. For the British attack broke through the Hindenburg Line, against odds of nearly three to two in force, before the Meuse-Argonne attack had drawn off any enemy divisions from its front. And the Meuse-Argonne attack failed to break through, with odds of five to one in force. Thus the event proved that there was no need to ease Haig's attack and that it was not possible to fulfill his idea of cutting off the German retreat by a converging advance toward the Ardennes and the lateral railway. And it also proved that Pershing was unduly optimistic of his troops' capacity to sweep rapidly through the German defenses. Yet, in justice to him, it must be emphasized that he had scant time to prepare the Meuse-Argonne attack and to shift his centre of gravity to the new sector; he was thus forced to use only the higher staffs and not the troops tried out at St. Mihiel, and to employ mainly fresh divisions for his Meuse-Argonne blow. Despite their gallantry, these paid heavily for their inexperience, if also for the system and the staple weapon on which their training was based. Their severe check was also due to the Germans' repetition of the method of elastic defense — with the real resistance some miles in the rear — for which the attackers were unprepared. Thus they ran into this cunningly woven belt of fire when their initial spurt was exhausted and their formation disordered.

Under such difficulties it was largely due to Pershing's driving force that the attack was sustained and continued to make headway, if slow, until October 14. He then handed over the command of the First Army to Liggett, giving Bullard command of the newly formed Second Army, under his higher control. If the loss was exorbitant, it was strategically balanced by the fact of drawing in many of the Germans' last reserves. It was also largely due to his drastic, even ruthless, action in changing commanders who had lacked driving force that the way was paved for the triumphant resumption of the advance on November 1.

Reviewing the course of the war's last phase, it would seem beyond doubt that Pershing was unfairly tried, that an exploitation of the St. Mihiel stroke by an advance toward Metz, with the "blooded" divisions and long-standing preparations which he used at St. Mihiel, would have made better progress than the Meuse-Argonne advance. Even so, however, it could hardly have made the rapid penetration which was essential to fulfill his strategic aim. Thus the ultimate verdict on his strategy, as on his training doctrine, must be that it was more idealistic than realistic. Like the French, in the early phase of the war, it foundered on the rock of machine guns. He thought that he was spreading a new gospel of faith when actually it was an old faith exploded. This was the one flaw in the great structure he had built.

It may even be said that he omitted but one factor from his calculations — German machine guns — and was right in all his calculations but one — their effect. It was the abrupt discovery by his troops of this omission which shook their initial trust in him, and led to some of the sweeping unjust post-war criticisms. This change of attitude was typified in a story which was widely told. In a column of American troops on the march a voice was heard saying, "Pershing says he'll take Metz if it costs a hundred thousand lives." Silence for a moment. Then another voice: "Ain't he a damned generous guy!"

Yet even this remark has an undercurrent of chastened yet grudging admiration which is a tribute both to the driving force of Pershing and to the fortitude of his men. He lacked the personal magnetism which can make men lay down their lives gladly — he was far from a Robert E. Lee. But he had the character which compelled men not only to die but to work — cursing him, perhaps, but respecting him. He was hard, but life had tried him hardly, and if he gave affection to few it was generous when given — to those who had shown themselves *men* by his high standard. When he visited the battlefields after the war he stood silent awhile before the monument on the mound at Montdidier dedicated to the 1st American Division.   At length, in a voice husky with emotion, he said, "That was the best damned division in *any* army."   It was a tribute from the heart.

As for his achievement, it is sufficient to say that there was perhaps no other man who would or could have built the structure of the American army on the scale he planned.   And without that army the war could hardly have been saved and could not have been won.